The Deciding Factor

The Deciding Factor

The Power of Analytics to Make Every Decision a Winner

Larry Rosenberger and John Nash
with Ann Graham

JOSSEY-BASS
A Wiley Imprint
www.josseybass.com

Published by Jossey-Bass
A Wiley Imprint
989 Market Street, San Francisco, CA 94103-1741—www.josseybass.com

Jossey-Bass books and products are available through most bookstores. To contact Jossey-Bass
directly call our Customer Care Department within the U.S. at 800-956-7739, outside the U.S.
at 317-572-3986, or fax 317-572-4002.

Jossey-Bass also publishes its books in a variety of electronic formats. Some content that appears
in print may not be available in electronic books.

Library of Congress Cataloging-in-Publication Data
Rosenberger, Larry, 1946-
    The deciding factor : the power of analytics to make every decision a winner / Larry Rosenberger
and John Nash with Ann Graham.
      p. cm.
Includes bibliographical references and index.
ISBN 978-0-470-39819-7 (cloth)
    1. Decision making. 2. Management. I. Nash, John, 1962- II. Graham, Ann, 1956
    July 22- III. Title.
HD30.23.R672 2009
658.4'03—dc22

2008051600

Printed in the United States of America
FIRST EDITION
HB Printing   10 9 8 7 6 5 4 3 2 1

Contents

Introduction

Whatever the circumstances—dire or trivial, clear-cut or complex—every decision is a choice between two or more actions that, for better or worse, lead to an outcome. *The Deciding Factor* is a book about how companies use decision management—the discipline and the technologies—to improve the outcomes of millions of operational decisions that affect a company's relationship with its customers and prospects.

In 2007 researchers predicted that by 2010 businesses and consumers worldwide would be spending $1.5 trillion annually on information technology hardware, software, and services.[1] At work, at home, at school, in our cars, at the beach—indeed, physically and virtually everywhere—our lives operate on continual streams of digital data. Displacing the paper trail is a digital trail, residing in computer databases, both private and public. There isn't a business or a consumer anywhere today that isn't touched by the trillions upon trillions of revealing bytes moving through wired and wireless, stationary and mobile information technologies.

All twenty-first-century corporations, no matter the industry or where or how they operate, therefore face the same challenge and opportunity: How can we create financial and customer *value* from unprecedented access to such huge amounts of digital data?

And the next big question is, what will companies *do* with this data to stimulate the next wave of business innovation? Can the executives of large corporations who focus on the future even envision what it might look like? As a leader of your corporation, can you?

These are the questions we thought about when we decided to write this book.

Data masters of the Internet, such as Amazon and Netflix, have made *analytics* and *algorithms* the hottest buzzwords in business, but how many C-level executives and line managers (unless they have an advanced degree in math or computer science) understand what analytics does? We have written *The Deciding Factor* not only to show executives why they should care but also to offer a different path to success in a digital world:

- It's not "all about the data."
- It's not "all about the math."
- It's not "all about the analytics."
- It's not "all about software technology."

Although all of those elements are important, successfully *using* all the data you mine and analyze with powerful software—data about your customers, your market, your industry, and your competition—really depends on the *decisions* you make. At the end of the day, what drives the results your company achieves are the millions of decisions your company makes that are informed by and in turn shape customer interactions and transactions every day. This is what we call *decision management*. As we will explain, analytics is part of decision management; the two are not synonymous.

For more than fifty years, the mathematicians, operations researchers, and computer scientists at our company, the Fair Isaac Corporation, have helped companies create business value by making better operational decisions. Our company is perhaps best known for the credit score product known as the FICO® score, which is based on our own proprietary algorithms to measure an individual's credit risk. FICO scores have become a standard tool used by consumer banks around the world to measure and evaluate consumer credit risk, for credit cards, bank lines of credit, mortgages, and insurance.

The Deciding Factor shows how leading companies in financial services industries and many other consumer industries—insurance, retail, health care, and consumer-packaged goods, among others—are using analytic techniques to predict customer behavior and then use that insight to make better operational decisions. When executed well, the actions from those analytically based decisions create more value for customers and more profit for companies.

But before we get caught up in analytics—and the "analytic techniques" and "analytically based decisions" mentioned in the previous paragraph—keep in mind that, in plain English, *analytics* is simply "a method of logical analysis." And *data* is "factual information (as measurements or statistics) used as a basis for reasoning, discussion, or calculation," according to *Webster's*. That's exactly what we're advocating in this book: how to use logical analysis based on *data* to make better decisions that will benefit both your business and your customers. Add *digital*—"information in numerical form that can be digitally transmitted or processed"—into the mix, and all together they form *decision management*.

The Deciding Factor features companies from around the world: Fair Isaac clients, such as Coca-Cola, Best Buy (the electronics retailer), Capital One (the financial services company that introduced the mass-customized credit card that is now an industry standard), ICICI (India's top retail bank that is going global), and Akbank (Turkey's leading consumer bank). We also look at companies we admire, such as Tesco (the third largest grocer and general merchandise retailer in the world), Netflix (the start-up company that blew away Blockbuster in DVD rentals), and Harrah's Entertainment (the world's largest gaming company). These are companies that are well known for their analytical prowess, but we also look at them as customer-driven decision makers.

Why This Book Is So Important Now

It's no accident that the information technology industry long ago chose the word *mining* to describe what companies aspire to do with their data. They knew data contained *gold,* and now that we are well into the digital age, companies are scrambling to figure out how they can get their piece of its value.

This book is long overdue. The data rush has been going on for some time now, though it seems only recently that executives and the strategy consultants who advise them have started to pay more attention to the importance of excellence in operations and the value of decision management technology. For example, Ian Davis, the chairman and CEO of McKinsey & Company, declared, "Long-gone is the day of gut instinct management styles . . . Today's business leaders are adopting algorithmic decision-making techniques and using highly sophisticated software to run their organizations. Scientific management is moving from a skill that creates competitive advantage to an ante that gives companies the right to play the game."[2]

Simon Kennedy and Dave Matheson, both senior partners with Boston Consulting Group, confirm the importance of *using* data:

> Given that this is the information age, why don't those who can benefit from existing data? Often the problem is that companies do have access, but don't recognize or appreciate what is in their grasp. With so many facts at hand about so many things—products, customers, sales, and more—it's easy to fail to connect the dots. Simply put, many companies have a competency issue in this area: very few have an advanced analytics capability or even a home for one. The operations side produces streams of data,

and IT ships it around but no one has the time, tools, or ability to take the data apart to find opportunities for advantage.[3]

Finally, C. K. Prahalad, one of the world's most influential management thinkers, believes that "As digitization permeates every aspect of business, every business is in effect, an e-business . . . While the hardware and connectivity part of this architecture can be delegated to IT departments and vendors, CEOs and line managers cannot delegate strategic decisions on the business applications, analytics capabilities, and data warehousing."[4]

In addition to the increasing attention analytics is getting from management thought leaders, media buzz is building: stories about data mining, business intelligence software, and analytics have always been standard fare in IT trade journals, but in the last three years more and more general business reporters in newspapers and magazines have picked up on stories about the way mathematics and computers are transforming how businesses operate and how we live. For example:

> Consumers and companies increasingly depend on a hidden mathematical world. Algorithms sound scary, of interest only to dome-headed mathematicians. In fact, they have become instruction manuals for a host of routine consumer transactions . . . from analyzing credit card transactions to deciding how to stack supermarket shelves, algorithms now underpin a large amount of everyday life.[5]

and this:

> Rising flows of data give companies the intelligence to home in on the individual customer. Internet marketers are the natural leaders, but traditional businesses are following suit. Gary W. Loveman, CEO of casino giant Harrah's Entertainment Inc. and a former Harvard B-school professor, has led the company to build individual profiles of millions of Harrah's customers. The models include gamblers' ages, gender, and ZIP codes, as

well as the amount of time they spent gambling and how much they won or lost. These data enable Harrah's to study gambling through a host of variables and to target individuals with offers, from getaway weekends to gourmet dining, calculated to maximize returns. In the last five years, Harrah's has averaged 22% annual growth, and its stock has nearly tripled.[6]

and this:

The desire to exploit computing and mathematical analytics is by no means new. In the 1960s and '70s, operations research combined computing and math mainly to make factory production work more efficient . . . most companies now have the tools to do the kind of competitive analytics that only a relative handful of elite companies could do in the past. "It's really starting to become mainstream,' says [Thomas H.] Davenport," co-author of a book on the topic: *Competing on Analytics: The New Science of Winning*. The entry barrier, he says, "is no longer technology, but whether you have executives who understand this."[7]

Who This Book Is For

Tom Davenport's comment echoes our sentiments exactly. Until recently, books about analytics (and books about decision management, although there aren't many of those) have been technical tomes, written for the mathematicians who dream up the equations, the IT professionals who embed the math in the software, and the operations experts who manage and try to improve business processes. Unlike them, *The Deciding Factor* is a strategy book that brings to life technical ideas about analytics for a broad management and strategy audience—both senior executives and rising executives.

The Deciding Factor can help managers in every industry, though the book does slightly emphasize financial services companies, because for two decades, many of the leading companies using analytics and decision management technologies have come from the consumer lending and banking sector. We have also chosen to focus on the demand side of business-to-consumer companies, rather than the supply-side applications for which analytics is also used. Analytics and decision management are spreading fast among consumer companies, in insurance, health care, and grocery and general merchandise retailing, because companies in these industries are flooded with transaction data that can be used to improve the customer experience, operating efficiency, and financial performance. So whatever industry you're working in, we're confident you have lots of untapped data that you can use to better your decisions and thus your competitive advantage. The book also offers a global perspective by featuring companies from the United States, Canada, Great Britain, Turkey, Brazil, Romania, and India.

Who We Are and Why We Wrote This Book

Fair Isaac is a global corporation serving clients in more than eighty countries, with revenues in 2008 of $745 million; it is one of the world's leading purveyors of mathematically based software used by corporations to automate operational decisions and to optimize profit and mitigate risk. Our market-leading software is used by many of the largest corporations in the world to improve their decisions in marketing, customer management, collections, and fraud management, with products such as the TRIAD® adaptive control system and Falcon® Fraud Manager.

We were motivated to write a book about the relationship between strategy and operations—and its link to customer value—because we worked as both executive leaders and technical implementers throughout our careers. Thinking about strategy and operations is a natural for both of us. Larry joined Fair Isaac in 1974 "as a kid out of school," as he likes to say, with degrees in physics from the MIT and in operations research from UC Berkeley. In 1991, he was chosen to succeed Bill Fair (one of Fair Isaac's cofounders) as CEO, a position he held until 1999, after which he went on to lead the R&D group, returning to his first passion: finding solutions to complex business process problems. In 2007 he became Fair Isaac's first research fellow.

John has an MBA from the University of Minnesota with a focus on information and decision sciences. Starting his career as a parts buyer for Rosemount Aerospace, a company that made precision flight sensors for the Space Shuttle and military aircraft, John moved on to Accenture, where he spent fourteen years working across retail, high-tech, manufacturing, and other industries, to help companies gain competitive advantage from technology. He was one of three founders of Accenture's global customer insight and CRM practices. An executive at Fair Isaac since 2002, he is currently the VP of strategy.

Together, we've worked with clients as diverse as retailers Best Buy, Lands' End, Lucky Stores (the grocery chain, not Lucky brand jeans), and SUPERVALU (the third largest food retailer in the United States); in the financial world, J. P. Morgan Chase, U.S. Bank, Wells Fargo Bank, GE Capital, HSBC, Banco Santander, ICICI, Sumitomo, Citi, Bank of America, Visa, MasterCard, and E*TRADE; and a range of other companies from Paul Revere insurance to Gateway computers.

We wrote this book to help executives understand the relationship between math and improving business processes, and to help managers and modelers use data, analytics, and software to make those decisions not *incrementally* better but *orders of magnitude* better.

To do this well, we believe executives need to think about the company's IT infrastructure not as technology to process data, as they have in the past, but as strategic resource for making better decisions. Furthermore, as IT infrastructures are streamlined and integrated, there is more opportunity to bring people and technology together to create a decision advantage. As MIT's Michael Schrage writes:

"The big-box retailers, Wal-Mart and Best Buy, are widely regarded as having superior analytic infrastructures. But they don't just hire the smartest 'quants.' They push them to make their mathematical tools accessible to others. They're constantly rethinking when mathematics should automate a decision, and when it should assist a decision maker."[8]

How This Book Can Help You

There are many management books for senior executives that focus on the periodic big-picture decisions that set the direction and objectives for the entire firm. In contrast, *The Deciding Factor* emphasizes how you can manage more effectively the quality of the millions of operational decisions your company makes every day—each of which can determine whether or not you achieve your corporate objectives. Even successful companies don't appreciate how much value can be created or lost in a single transaction, and how the cumulative effects of bad or careless operational decisions harm performance. For example, in the credit card industry it is well documented that companies have accepted losses from defaults of between 6 and 7 percent on annual receivables, adding up to billions of dollars.

Decision management is most applicable to high-volume, repeatable operational decisions. However, these decision management principles are *not* applicable to certain types of decision problems, namely:

- Highly collaborative, interactive team decisions, such as those that a team of engineers need to make regarding the design of a bridge.
- Corporate decisions that are singular or rarely repeated, such as deciding whether to expand in certain countries or to acquire another company.

Instead, *The Deciding Factor* focuses on how business-to-consumer companies—in consumer lending and banking, retailing, consumer packaged goods, insurance, health care, and mobile telecom industries—are making significant progress in applying decision management to:

- Use predictions of consumer behavior to grow the value of customer relationships (in other words, to attract, grow, and retain profitable customers)
- Make operational decision making more profitable, through effective use of voluminous customer data—and despite the increasing complexity and shifting dynamics of the business environment
- Increase the efficiency of decisions through automation, while simultaneously lowering risks and raising revenues

In other words, this book can help you serve your customers better and make more money. And who doesn't want that? As you begin this book, we ask you to keep in mind these key ideas:

- *Many managers responsible for "strategy" underestimate the effect that operational decisions have on strategy outcomes.* Indeed, salespeople, customer service reps, logistics managers, and marketing managers make decisions all the time. The quality, precision, and strategic forethought of decisions made throughout an organization have vital consequences for the overall success of corporate strategy.

- *Companies are not profit maximizers; they are constrained profit seekers.* The process of making business decisions almost always involves trade-offs between multiple competing objectives. We all know that what's good for shareholders may not be good for customers or employees, but we don't always acknowledge this. When a bank's marketing department sends credit card solicitations to people who are behind on their payments on an existing card, they are undermining the collection department's efforts to reduce delinquencies. When cost cutting degrades the customer experience, how much business value is lost even if short-term profitability goes up? Decision management makes the trade-offs visible.

- *You don't have to do the math to use it anymore.* Through automation and the distributed computing infrastructures, now operations research and analytic engineers, mathematicians, and computer specialists are not the only ones who can create business value. From the boardroom to the front line, executives and managers are using analytical insights to guide their decisions.

- *Companies get more business value from customer data when they don't try to squeeze the most profit they can out of every customer transaction.* They manage data to boost profitability by adding value to and strengthening the relationship over time.

We hope that you enjoy this book as much as we enjoyed writing it, as it truly is a wonderful story, given that there is both social and economic value in what we do. The social benefit comes when decisions are made on a much more objective and fair basis; for example, in responsible lending and responsible borrowing. Given the increasing complexities of financial systems and the global economy, there has never been a better time to apply mathematics and technology to ensure that decisions are fact-based, systematic, and transparent. The economic benefits will become more obvious as you read the case examples in the chapters to come, and we believe there are endless additional benefits to be gained when these decision management principles are put into practice by leaders with the right insight and creativity.

The Deciding Factor

1

FROM INTUITION TO ALGORITHMS

A Brief History of Using Analytics to Make Better Decisions

Late on a November night in 2006, along New York City's Bruckner Expressway in the South Bronx, a solid azure blue, brightly lit new billboard declared, in a single line of bold white block text:

THE ALGORITHM KILLED JEEVES.

The billboard stood out among the others hawking car dealers, reality TV shows, and sex clubs. Although it wasn't hard to get the "whodunit?" message, the billboard's sponsor was a mystery. A quick search, though, revealed that it was Ask.com, the search engine owned by the website conglomerate IAC Search and Media, Inc. Apparently its marketers had decided that a billboard along the Bruckner—the roadway home to the suburbs for the search engine's target user—would be a good place to announce that the dapper info-butler Jeeves had been dismissed for a better and faster model: the algorithm. The billboard was meant to draw attention to Ask.com's new and improved website-ranking algorithm called ExpertRank, and to contrast it with archrival Google's search algorithm, PageRank.

Geeky highway billboards, sponsored by cheeky web search engine marketers, are certainly signs of the times. Mathematical moguls are making vast fortunes by differentiating models that compute complex equations with extraordinary speed and precision. "Once upon a time, the most valuable secret formula in American business was Coca-Cola's. Today it's Google's master algorithm," wrote Randall Stross, author of multiple books on internet-era moguls, in his *New York Times* column "Digital Domain."[1] An algorithm is a set of mathematically derived instructions to accomplish a defined task. Algorithms running on powerful computer networks are not just a part of the digital revolution; they are spawning a revolution in how business decisions are managed and made.

Of course, the seeds for this revolution—and for the digital technology that enables companies to apply such mathematical rigor to operational decision making—were planted long ago.

"Predicting short-term changes or shocks is often a fool's errand. But forecasting long-term directional change is possible by identifying trends through an analysis of deep history rather than of the shallow past. Even the Internet took more than 30 years to become an overnight phenomenon,"[2] writes Ian Davis, chairman and CEO of McKinsey & Company.

Today's digital data management discipline known as *analytics* began with the first mainframe computers in the 1950s. In this chapter, we look back over the past sixty years, not because the history of analytics and decision management is so fascinating (though much of it is, as you'll see), but to show you how far companies have come in using computers and analytics to achieve all of the following goals:

- To sort through the enormous amount of data they have about their businesses
- Which helps them make better decisions about serving their customers
- Which in turn improves the value they offer their customers as well as their overall profitability

If you share these goals, read on.

The Pioneers of Decision Management

Long before marketers were posting arcane mathematical terms on highway billboards, business pioneers were using math and computers to make better decisions. These business visionaries promoted a union of computing power, powerful equations, and brainpower to achieve business insights from deep and diverse analysis of operational data.

The First Use of Computers to Improve Decision Making

Back in the 1950s, at MIT's Sloan School of Management, computer scientist Jay Forrester argued that a large corporation is a complex social system far too abstract for human beings to manage effectively without the aid of computers. He asserted that we literally *need* technology to understand the relationships and interactions among people in big organizations. In 1961, Forrester published *Industrial Dynamics*, his seminal book on systems dynamics—an analytical, problem-solving methodology he developed that employs computer-based simulations to help managers visualize and understand cause-and-effect relationships in decision making and business processes that would otherwise be invisible and inestimable.

Forrester also used the term *mental models* to describe how people tend to make decisions based on instinct and interpretation rather than on fact. Forrester believed that management decisions based only on mental models and human judgments are inferior to decisions derived from computer models that can represent complex relationships and predict outcomes that the human mind can't. In the 1970s, Donnella

> Management decisions based only on mental models are inferior to decisions derived from computer models that can represent complex relationships and predict outcomes that the human mind can't.

Meadows, a protégé of Forrester's from MIT, applied his theories of systems dynamics to produce a global model for the Club of Rome that was the basis for the controversial book *Limits to Growth*, which predicted all of the long-term trends in population growth, economics, and the state of the earth's environment that have since come to pass. Another Forrester protégé, Peter Senge, popularized systems dynamics in a management context with his book *The Fifth Discipline*. Decision management arises from the same notions of systems complexity.

Whereas Forrester advocated for more computer-guided management of business systems in the 1950s and early '60s in Cambridge, the International Business Machine Corporation—now known simply as IBM—was making its transition from punch card processors to electronic computers. Thomas J. Watson, Jr., bet the company's future on the thinking machines his father had dismissed as too expensive and unreliable. Taking charge in 1952, the younger Watson hired hundreds of electrical engineers to start designing the first mainframe computers. Little did he know that this decision to commit IBM's business machine vision to computers would kick-start the information technology revolution in business and the beginnings of decision management in large corporations.

Fair Isaac's Formative Days with Decisions Management

At about the same time, in California, two young process management scientists—William R. Fair, an engineer, and Earl J. Isaac, a mathematician—were starting their careers in the new field of operations research. Then, as now, operations research involved applying advanced mathematics and statistics using computers to analyze complex operational business processes to improve the process through better decisions. Bill and Earl met in 1953 at the Stanford Research Institute (SRI), a think tank that primarily did operations research for the military. Bill and

Earl spent their days as operations research scientists at SRI, helping the U.S. Defense Department figure out how to contain the destruction of an atomic bomb. They created elaborate mathematical models to run on SRI's behemoth computer in order to answer basic questions. Their concern was not how to build missiles and atomic weapons, but how to operate them. How do you carry them? Where do you aim? How close to the target?

Bill had studied engineering at the California Institute of Technology in the 1940s. During World War II, he had been a radar technical representative for Sperry Gyroscope and had served in the Pacific with the Marine Corps. As a civilian, he also applied his engineering skills repairing night fighter radars on aircraft carriers. After the War, Fair finished his schooling at Berkeley and Stanford. Isaac, who studied mathematics at the U.S. Naval Academy and UCLA, had been part of the team that developed the initial programming for one of the first electrical computers—the U.S. Bureau of Standards Electronic Eastern Automatic Computer, otherwise known as SEAC.

As Bill progressed in his career at SRI and his analysis of operational processes for missile systems and atomic weapons, he became convinced the research they were performing for the military could be just as valuable to *businesses*. Why couldn't the operational analysis performed for the Defense Department be applied in other contexts, like corporations serving consumer product and service markets? He visualized the corporation as a sensitive machine similar to the radar systems he had repaired during the war. Like Jay Forrester, he believed that managers needed computers and mathematics to solve tough operational problems and to make consistently better managerial choices.

Bill founded SRI's first nonmilitary operations research practice, and he asked Earl to join his group. It wasn't long before the independent and ambitious duo decided to leave SRI to form their own consulting business for the private sector. In an interesting turn of fate, Bill had taken half his courses at the business school while working toward a master's in engineering at Stanford. Combining Bill's head for business with Earl's rare computer talents and passion for mathematics, in 1956 they each chipped in $400 to start Fair, Isaac and Company, Inc. According to Fair Isaac lore, Bill and Earl decided to combine their own last names to come up with a name for the company, but they were concerned that "Isaac Fair" sounded like one person and "Fair Isaac" sounded like a used car salesman. As Fair tells the story, they "settled on the lesser of two evils." Bill Fair was among the attendees at the First International Conference on Operations Research in 1957, just after they named their new company.

Bill Fair and Earl Isaac founded Fair Isaac because they believed, as did their business-minded engineering and mathematician peers, that the operational processes of corporations conceal a treasure trove of information to help managers run better companies. For an organization to be the best, its operational management decisions must be methodical and data-driven— not just guided by gut feelings and consensus. Their vision was to create computer-based mathematical tools for use by corporations to sharpen operational decision making and make process management the foundation for achieving consistently better business results. Fair and Isaac knew they could do the math and the analysis. The only glitch was that computing technology was still too primitive, too scarce, and too expensive.

In the 1950s—when men wore hats, not headphones, and computers were the size of a tank—few companies even used computers or would have known what to do with it if they had one. Even Bill and Earl didn't have their own a computer, so they worked out a time-share deal with the Standard Oil Company of California (today's Chevron) to use its mainframe during nonpeak evening hours to conduct their research. The SEAC machine Earl had worked with had been a physical monster with a grand total of only 512 words of high-speed memory. Earl contributed to the development of many of the early computer languages, but his thorough grounding in machine language and even in bit programming, along with his natural talent for the subject, gave him an understanding of the nature of the computer that was equaled by few people in the world at that time.

Fair Isaac Takes Off with the U.S. Credit Card Industry

It took the fledgling company almost three years, but in 1958, Fair and Isaac and Earl Follett—a fellow mathematician, alumni of SRI, and Fair Isaac's first employee—identified consumer credit as a process in which they could put their ideas to work. By the 1960s, as more business operations started to be computerized, and credit cards became an accepted alternative to cash, suddenly it was possible for companies to capture data on customers' behavior. When people pay cash for goods and services, it is an "anonymous" transaction. The only record of the transaction is the receipt. For the first time, companies could capture transaction-level data on masses of people.

Credit Scoring Drives Better Decisions and Growth in Consumer Lending. Credit card issuers were interested in seeing trends (that is, what people were buying or not buying). They were even more interested in knowing more about how to manage the risks of mass market lending. Fair Isaac invented the credit score to help lenders analyze each applicant's credit risk while handling many more applications than they ever had before. The credit score was the first big application of analytics for Fair Isaac, and the beginning of what the company today calls decision management.

A few companies had dabbled in business applications of scoring as early as World War II, but none thought of applying it to consumer lending. As operations research experts, Bill and Earl were familiar with statistical analytic techniques such as multivariate analysis and logistic regression. Earl Follet knew how to apply these concepts to managing credit risk. When

Fair Isaac's first credit scoring model was introduced in 1958, it was the first to use the historical data being captured by finance companies to predict a person's creditworthiness based on their past behavior. The model produced a score, based on analysis of specific sets of numbers related to variables such as a person's bank balance and payment records. The credit score was a far better predictor of a customer's ability to pay back a loan than any decision a banker could make on his own, even if he knew the applicant personally.

Using Predictive Analytics to Make Better Decisions About Customers' Behavior. Predictive analytics is a way to make connections between the past and the future, using historical data to predict future events. Simply put, it's the study of how what you know at the time you make a decision relates to what you don't know: what will happen in the future. The credit-scoring model was built based on variables such as these:

- Income
- Bank account balances
- Outstanding credit
- Payment history
- Time with present employer

These variables were vetted as highly predictive of a consumer's creditworthiness.

Credit scoring models, and the type of predictive analytics Fair Isaac is known for generally, quantify the patterns and relationships among dozens of variables. Every credit application had all the data needed to build the model. A single score could convey the risk associated with a person's future payment behavior and the person's risk profile relative to the behavior of many other people. Using mathematics to predict the behavior of masses of consumers was a revolutionary concept when first proposed. Today, credit scoring is a cornerstone of lending processes, and other analytic applications using data on consumer behavior are revolutionizing mass advertising, direct marketing, and customer service—to name a few business processes that are spawning new, creative analytic applications.

Fair Isaac's first foray into credit scoring, however, took more than a decade to take off. In fact, Fair Isaac didn't sell a credit-scoring system to a bank's credit card division until 1970. The first general-purpose FICO® score was not developed until 1989. It took time for business attitudes and technology to change.

In 1958, Bill and Earl sent letters to about fifty major credit grantors—mainly consumer banks and finance companies—in the United States asking for a meeting to explain credit scoring and its value. Only one institution replied. More often than not, business clients showed little interest in operational insights. All they wanted was to install their first computer and get it running. The idea of the computer as a tool for analytic computation was way ahead of what business people were thinking.

Still, the timing for scoring was right, because it coincided with growth in nonbanking businesses that were offering credit and capturing the data. Early charge cards (which were metal, not plastic) had been around since the 1930s. By the late 1950s, consumer use of cards rather than cash was growing, and metal charge cards were being replaced by the plastic credit cards we use today. Although Fair Isaac's first credit-scoring system sale was to American Investment—a finance company based in St. Louis, Missouri—banks were initially reluctant to adopt the new credit-scoring approach.

On the other hand, national department store chains—such as JCPenney, Montgomery Ward, and Sears, Roebuck—were intrigued by the idea of a systematic way to grow their store charge card bases at a time when few people had credit cards. Montgomery Ward, one of the first U.S. national department store chains, was one of Fair Isaac's best and most progressive clients. As credit cards took off in other consumer service industries (gasoline retail and hotels), more businesses became interested in credit scoring.

But the information management tools and processes were still basic. Before oil companies and department stores began automating their accounts receivables and billing processes, customer account records were stored on ledger cards coded from handwritten account information. Ledger cards were created and maintained using the National Cash Register (NCR) Company's billing machines—which had one keypad for debits and another for credits—to calculate balance, finance charges, and so on. The ledger cards, posted manually, listed information about each customer's charge purchases—the dollar amounts, what they bought, and the date.

As late as the mid-1970s, Fair Isaac staffers had to spend days in their retail store client's backroom credit card operations so they could gather the data to build their models. They used a microfilm camera to photograph the information from the ledger cards. Larry recalls that during the summer of 1974 he drove from store to store, photographing thousands of records and praying the images would come out so that he would not have to go back and do it all again. While onsite, he also listened to the store's collection department staff calling delinquent customers. He recalls that it was eye-opening to see the reality of the process Fair Isaac was trying to improve.

Through the mid-twentieth century in the United States, the granting of credit occurred only between businesses. The process was completely based on human judgments, including conclusions that would be socially and legally unacceptable by today's standards. (From the 1920s to the 1930s, merchants relied first on gender and race to assess their suppliers, along with "character traits" such as honesty, punctuality, and sobriety.) It wasn't until the 1940s that it was possible to collect real and accurate data on an individual's actual credit and payment history, which turned out to be fundamental predictors of a person's reliability as a user of credit.

Although there are consumer advocates today who still question whether there is racial bias in credit scoring processes, Fair Isaac, from the start, literally took prejudice out of the equations. In the early years, some lenders balked. Earl Isaac refused one banker's insistence that race be a variable in their scorecard. Another lender put a secret code on loan application forms from minority applicants. Scoring killed this practice. (In fact, after the Equal Opportunity Act was adopted in the mid-1970s, some lenders were ordered to use scoring in their decision-making process.)

Diners Club and Amex Issue the First Expense Account Cards. The big surge in general-purpose credit cards began after World War II. In 1950, department store baron Alfred Bloomingdale and his partners Frank X. McNamara and Ralph Snyder created the Diner's Club Card for use at select restaurants and stores. Diner's Club was the first credit card aimed at getting a piece of the travel and entertainment expense accounts of young and prospering veterans who were now ambitious corporate organization men. In 1958, the same year Bill and Earl brought the credit score to market, American Express, best known then for inventing the traveler's check, issued its first card aimed at businessmen.

Carte Blanche Takes a Tiny Step in Tracking Delinquent Accounts. The same year, Conrad Hilton, of the hotel chain, also jumped into the burgeoning credit card market targeting prosperous organization men. With a grand panjandrum's flair, he named the company's card Carte Blanche. Like other credit card promoters of the day, Hilton aggressively marketed the card, but he wasn't terribly analytical in his approach. The company sent the Carte Blanche card to every guest who stayed at a Hilton hotel and signed up any merchant who was willing to accept the card. To compete with Diner's and Amex, Hilton agreed to take a lower (4 percent) share of each charge, and he was willing to issue cards to people whose payment histories did not make the grade with other card companies. But this strategy for growth was a nonstarter for all the new card companies. Diners Club also tried to compete with other card companies by reducing its credit standards, but it abandoned that strategy after default rates rose to an unacceptable level.

Fair Isaac did work for Hilton in the early 1960s, but Carte Blanche was not a scoring client. Fair Isaac was brought in to design a billing system. No one inside the company had given any thought to any aspect of managing the billing process for the card. Bill and Earl found out just how bad the situation was when they arrived at Hilton's offices in 1961 to start working. They opened a closet door and found stacks of mail sacks on the floor, filled with *hundreds of thousands of dollars*! There was no system to manage the money, much less a way to manage the enormous volume of data and transactions that the Carte Blanche credit cards were generating.

Earl used punch-card equipment he had on hand for another client to design and install a billing system in a week. Hilton executives were dazzled. They told Earl this was the closest thing to a miracle any of them had ever seen, but apparently this feat wasn't enough. Unfortunately, Hilton's billing snafu was reported in the press: *Time* magazine ran a story called "Carte Blank" in April of 1961, which revealed that Hilton would lose $4 million for the 1961 fiscal year (which ended that month). The reason, as Carte Blanche officials told *Time*, was "our unsatisfactory collection experience."[3]

Two months earlier, Conrad Hilton and several associates had pumped $5 million into the corporation to cover credit card losses. To reduce its risk exposure, the company tightened its credit checks and created new requirements for cardholder applicants: "25 years of age, at least $7,200 in annual salary, and an established pattern of wise and consistent use of credit."

By then Hilton also had an IBM computer system in place, which checked daily on the state of the accounts and sent out reminders to delinquent cardholders. Carte Blanche's credit checks and automated account status monitoring were the first steps in using transaction data to put more science behind the management of their marketing and billing processes. Rudimentary as it was, Carte Blanche's decision to send these reminders to delinquent cardholders was early decision management. Today's technology, applied in a bank collection process, automates these kinds of decisions and can create strategies to improve responsiveness from millions of individual customers.

Citibank Invites Everyone to Join, Without Assessing Any Credit Risk. When Citibank decided to take its Citicard credit card business national under former CEO John Reed's leadership in the 1970s, the bank actually mailed offers by using lists from phone books across the country. The losses on this direct mail campaign were in the millions, but Reed shrugged his shoulders and said it was just a cost of building the business quickly. But they never did it again, until a senior executive with a background in analytical modeling stepped up to articulate a discipline for balancing risk and reward in acquiring new customers.

Mass Marketing and Mass Consumer Data Emerge

Mass marketing of credit cards changed the customer growth possibilities for banks and for consumer lending generally. Not only did credit cards make it possible to reach millions of more people with a personal credit product, but it also gave card issuers a more direct way to track and influence their customers' spending. In the consumer lending business, the credit card and the credit scoring process supported the financial services industry's growth from its traditional base in single hometown banks and savings and loans to national branch networks.

Consumer lending in the United States, before and after World War II, was part of the fabric of cities and towns and communities. The saga of the greedy Mr. Potter and the hero George Bailey in the American holiday classic *It's a Wonderful Life* set its timeline from the 1920s through the 1940s. Local bankers were pillars of the community who socialized with many of their customers. By the 1970s, though, national consumer finance companies, such as Household and Beneficial Finance, had several thousand branches scattered in towns around the country. They strove for local trust and the personal touch, running radio spots with neighborly slogans, such as Household Finance's "You're good with us" or Beneficial Finance's "With Beneficial, you're good for more." When you walked into a local office and filled out an application for a loan, a branch manager—who also happened to be the credit officer—reviewed your application, sized you up, and made a decision whether or not to give you a loan. In other words, the marketing and customer experience was supposed to be very personal, which is a nice way to run a small-town general store or bank but not a very practical or profitable way to run a national retail bank system. For that, banks needed a systematic way to raise the volume and speed up the processing of loan applications and manage the risk in lending to more people. Credit scoring was just the system to tackle all these new challenges.

Today, credit scoring is a standard tool to manage credit, and it is used throughout a variety of industries; for example:

- All retail banks use credit scores to manage everything from loan approvals and interest rate levels to lines of credit for a wide variety of lending products and for millions of customers and prospects.
- Insurance companies also use scores in deciding individual customer eligibility and which services to offer.
- Health care organizations are beginning to use scores to determine who they should pursue to collect delinquent fees and who they should write off.

ASAP: The First Automated System for Processing Credit Applications. It took so long for credit scores to catch on in part because computer technology still had to catch up to the vision of mass automated decision making. Right up until the early 1970s, not only were credit applications submitted and reviewed *on paper*, but scorecards were also deployed *in a manual environment*. We take for granted today how pervasive automation is in businesses and many other aspects of our lives, but if you were working a few decades ago (as *we* were), you'll recall offices with typewriters and adding machines instead of a computer on every desk.

So it was a groundbreaking achievement when Earl Isaac came up with the idea to use a computer to automate the processing

> We could use scientific methodology to help us make decisions, and we could use information technology to help provide mass customization.

of credit applications. He wrote the software for a system called the Automated Strategic Applications Processing (ASAP) system, and he created a computer language known as PROSPER.

In 1972, Wells Fargo Bank bought its first ASAP system. The first ASAP seems unfathomable today. The product ran on a Data General Nova minicomputer that was hardly a mini machine—actually it was one step away from the data processing center full of refrigerator-sized mainframe computers. The Nova had only 8 kilobytes of memory (compare *that* to the memory of 1 to 2 gigabytes in a typical laptop today) and a prechip computer-processing unit that measured 14 by 14 inches (today's CPUs are 33 by 33 millimeters, a tiny fraction of an inch).

Automated loan application processing became a mainstay product for Fair Isaac; we developed versions for mainframes, then PCs, and then the Internet, as each technology advanced. But the real significance was this: with ASAP, Fair Isaac entered the software business, and the company found that the automation of the loan approval process was as valuable as the mathematical formulas used to score applications. The move from handwritten accounting books and ledger cards to the automation of the analytic models was the key to mass-scale lending and making millions of consumer loans.

Improving Credit Account Decision Managements via Adaptive Control. Larry Rosenberger joined Fair Isaac in 1974, fresh out of school. With undergraduate and graduate degrees in physics from MIT and the University of California at Berkeley, and a Ph.D. in operations research from Berkeley, Larry was eager to put his education to work. As he saw it, Fair Isaac's mission to help companies analyze and improve decision making in complex operational processes would offer him a lifetime career of study in systems dynamics as well as an endless supply of interesting business puzzles to solve.

Indeed, one of Fair Isaac's most important credit scoring technology innovations started with just such a problem, and some scribbling on the back of an ink blotter. The problem was this: in the mid-1980s, banks weren't buying behavior scorecards that measured customer risk after a loan was booked, because the scorecards were too hard to install and use in their client's computer systems. Bill Fair illustrated how control theory might be applied to solve this problem, and Larry ran with the idea.

Both Larry and Bill had a sophisticated understanding of control theory, using both engineering and mathematics to analyze systems. Simply said, in any system inputs can be controlled to obtain the desired output. Larry saw in Bill's drawings the opportunity for Fair Isaac to go beyond just creating the algorithms for scorecards, to building an automated system in which the scorecards would operate. The technology was named *adaptive control.* Chapter Four will explain adaptive control in detail, but for now, all you need to know is that adaptive control changed the way credit card issuers manage decisions such as these:

- Adjusting a customer's line of credit so that the risk of delinquency is controlled as the line of credit is increased

- Accepting or declining a credit card used at a checkout coun-
  ter or online (for example, a customer can make a purchase
  over the credit limit, if automated analytics approve it)

In both decisions, the automation of the analytics works to
optimize profitability and minimize risk for the business and
to increase convenience and good will for the customer.

The Scoring Tool Digs into Credit Bureau Data. In 1989,
another big breakthrough for the credit industry came when Fair
Isaac installed its first-general purpose credit bureau scorecards
at Equifax, one of the three major credit bureaus in the United
States. With these scorecards, any lender could measure the
credit risk of an applicant or current customer— at a cost of just
pennies per transaction. The huge amounts of data the credit
bureaus had amassed made these scores more accurate and useful in making credit management decisions.

Capital One's Customer Card Revolution. The science and
creativity of predictive analytics and automated decisions gained
momentum in the credit card industry at the beginning of the
1990s, as "plastic" became as ubiquitous as cash. For example,
consider the difference thirty years made to the credit industry:

- In 1970, only 6 percent of American householders carried
  a credit card balance.
- By 2000, 40 percent of householders carried one or more
  credit cards.[4]

In the 1990s, all leading credit card companies, such as
Capital One, First USA, and MBNA, were using information technology to churn out new credit card products and
supercharge revenue growth and growth in market share while
keeping the lid on costs. MBNA and Capital One stood out
for their focus on customer profitability. Both were interested

in consumer behavior, but their approaches were very different. MBNA invented the "affinity" card, a product cobranded with professional associations. MBNA targeted segments they believed would be receptive and lucrative, such as those for doctors, lawyers, and university alumni. They did not use analytics. Capital One did and created the first mass-customized marketing and customer service in the industry while managing the profitability of each customer relationship.

Like Bill Fair and Earl Isaac, Richard Fairbank and his partner Nigel Morris came from the management consulting world, and they had the mathematical skills and a vision of what computers could do with equations to help managers make better decisions. They coined the term *information-based strategy* to describe their pairing of scientific management with information technology.

Here is how Richard Fairbank—chairman, CEO, and cofounder of Capital One—described their operational vision for his company: "When we started this company, we saw two revolutionary opportunities. We could use scientific methodology to help us make decisions, and we could use information technology to help provide mass customization."[5]

Capital One took testing, learning, and automation of analytical models in retail banking to a new level—which was why the company was profiled in *Fast Company* magazine, detailing extraordinary results like these:[6]

- In 1994, "Cap One" was an adventurous spin-off of Signet Bank, a small regional consumer bank that was based in the small town of Springfield, Virginia. By 2005—only eleven years later—Cap One had become the 115th largest company in the S&P 500, with annual revenues of $10 billion.
- "Capital One has enough information on consumers to fill the hard drives of more than 200,000 personal computers . . . It uses that information much as a physicist uses a particle accelerator: Cap One analysts and product managers come up with

an idea for a product, bounce the data a bit, test it, tweak it, and launch it as fast as possible."

- In 1998, the company performed twenty-eight thousand tests of new products, new advertising, approaches, new markets, and new business models.
- In 1998, the company offered six thousand kinds of credit cards, each with slightly different terms, requirements, and benefits, and each requiring a slightly different monthly statement.

> The decision-making potential in the volume of data accessible to all businesses has become a deciding factor in their success.

In the early days of direct marketing of credit cards, companies made a single fixed offer, and they randomly searched for people who would accept the offer. In contrast, Cap One mined dozens of databases to design thousands of slightly varied credit cards. Then the company targeted each design for precisely defined customer segments. Each segment had different means and tastes, but all had a high probability of signing up and becoming a profitable customer. Consider the following wildly different examples:

- A suburban family man in his forties, with a six-figure income, and a taste for fine cars and wine, might get a $20,000 credit line with an affinity card comarketed with Mercedes-Benz, with no annual fee.
- In contrast, a typical offer to a recent college graduate might be for a $200 credit line with a $20 annual fee.

Computer systems and technology tools enable companies to apply math and statistical disciplines to decision making with an exactness and scale that Bill Fair and Earl Isaac couldn't have imagined back when they were working with Hilton and grappling with the sacks of cash stuffed into closets. Cap One's information-based strategy, as applied in the company's call center operations, was a state-of-the-art advancement for the credit card industry nearly a decade ago, and it remains so today. The fast, interactive customer environment created through Cap One's early analytics was a leading indicator of how company and customer relationships would evolve in the age of the Internet. Like all retail banks, Cap One was caught up in the subprime mortgage crisis of 2008, but over the years its competence in analytics has helped the company weather economic downturns and industry volatility better than competitors. We will talk more about its recent innovations in analytics in Chapter Four.

Different Companies Use Analytics Differently

Companies competing on analytics typically differentiate their algorithms. But sometimes companies using the same models may decide on very different business strategies.

Allstate versus State Farm versus Progressive

Consider the role analytics played in the American auto insurance market over the last fifteen years. State Farm Insurance Company, founded in 1922, and Allstate Insurance Corporation, founded in 1931, are well known to American drivers. A third company, Progressive Insurance, has been selling auto insurance almost as long (it was founded in 1937), but before the 1990s it was not the household name the other two companies were. Today, Progressive is the third largest insurer in the United States (13.8 billion auto insurance policies sold in 2007). Progressive also positions itself as an industry innovator. In the 1990s, its service at the scene of the accident was ahead of the industry. In 2007, Progressive became the first insurance company to offer coverage for injuries suffered by pets in automobile accidents. It pays up to $500 for veterinary bills for dogs and cats. The protection is included at no additional charge for customers who buy collision coverage.

Another example of Progressive's innovation has to do with a counterintuitive market it was able to cultivate through the use of analytics. Historically, most auto insurance companies used the same predictive model to assign risk to drivers and the same criteria to identify bad drivers. (Hence, "If you have these characteristics, you are 90 percent likely to have a claim.")

State Farm and Allstate took that information and decided to set pricey premiums to discourage people with bad driving records from applying. This was the strategy: charge customers even more than necessary to make a profit. Progressive took the same behavioral information and tried to attract drivers rejected by their competitors. Before they even did the modeling, they had a hypothesis that they could make money from "bad" drivers. Then they used analytics to find a policy price just slightly below State Farm and Allstate but high enough to make a profit on customers who were likely to submit a claim.

Progressive used segmentation analytics to identify bad drivers, and a scoring model to differentiate the best of the worst from the worst (a 600 score is different from 550 and very different from 500). The other insurance companies lumped together all bad drivers (for example, any applicant with a score below 600).

Progressive's new customer growth went through the roof. Once the company dominated the bad driver market, Progressive diversified into more standard and preferred risk segments. The lesson: you can't intuitively price something precisely without analytics. Yet this is also an approach that combines scientific method and intuition. This ability to differentiate services and pricing and to meet a market need that other companies do not see is one important reason why analytics is such a powerful resource for gaining a competitive advantage.

Progressive may have had better statisticians than the other insurance companies, and they may have built a slightly better model, but that was not the deciding factor in their success. It was the decision to take a precisely calculated risk to go after those people with scores below 600 when other companies stayed away.

Big Companies Have Big Data Sets

Automakers and apparel makers, beverage makers and appliance makers, electronics makers, luxury hotels, banks, grocers, discount general merchandise retailers, and direct mail marketers have all chased the dream of using consumer data and analytics to identify new markets and do one-to-one marketing, mass customization, and personalization of products and shopping experiences, with varying degrees of success. Now they have the volume of data accessible to make the models more useful, because more data is being generated and the cost and complexity of collecting and storing data are no longer hurdles. Plus, processing is getting faster and faster, simply because computers are connected.

Cap One's cofounder Nigel Morris, speaking to Ann Graham in 2007, summed it up well: "Big companies now have big data sets on consumers so they have the raw materials to work with and that is a big asset . . . People can point to the insurance company, Progressive, and Harrah's, the casino company, and Capital One, and they can say, these companies have really leveraged this kind of information to create powerful consumer-based models. They are beacons that give other companies confidence that it might make sense for them to build this capability, too."

Even with the problems caused by using analytics and automation to extend credit to more and more people, there is no question that more people who qualify for credit and benefit from it have access to all types of credit products today. Not only has credit scoring made lending processes more efficient, but it has also made them more democratic and objective.

The credit score is a simple mathematical way for a lender to make sure its terms are met, or at least reduce its exposure to consumer default risk, by selecting data that are predictors of a person's creditworthiness. In theory, this eliminates human bias from the process. Of course, in practice mathematicians still select the criteria to be used in the model. Credit scoring is not a perfect science, nor is any analytic model. As Kurt Gödel—a twentieth-century logician, mathematician, and philosopher—said, "Mathematics is perfect, but it is not complete."

We've presented a bit of the recent history of consumer credit in the United States to demonstrate the role that computer-based analytics and automated decision making played in the twentieth century to dramatically increase the scale, speed, and quality of a single business process: consumer lending. Working with mere millions of kilobytes (one kilobyte is equal to the amount of data stored on an antiquated 3.5-inch floppy disk) and megabytes (one megabyte equals a pickup truck filled with paper), back in the 1970s Fair Isaac and our clients made analytics a catalyst for business innovation. Indeed, Harvard Business School's Clayton M. Christensen has called the development of credit scoring, which subsequently led to automated credit approvals that accelerated and transformed the credit card industry, one of the top seventy-five disruptive business innovations of the twentieth century.[7]

How Analytics Is Being Used in the Twenty-First Century

The science of predicting consumer behavior and the art of using those predictions, which Fair and Isaac envisioned when they began building their business thirty years ago, is blossoming in the digital age.

The ability to use data to predict consumer behavior, and identify and differentiate markets, becomes more powerful as the volume of data grows. In 2004, Wal-Mart's data warehouse reached 500 terabytes (one terabyte equals fifty thousand trees made into paper and printed). Data flows on the Internet are now reaching into the exabyte range. In 2008, the Discovery Institute projected that by 2015 internet protocol-based data traffic in the United States will reach an annual total of 1,000 exabytes. Two exabytes equals the total volume of written information generated worldwide annually. Five exabytes is all the words ever spoken by human beings.[8]

As we noted earlier, the costs of collecting and storing data are falling steadily as processing power increases. Chris Anderson (editor in chief of *Wired* magazine and author of *The Long Tail*) has noted that data management costs are falling so fast that they are already too low to measure: "The cost of storing or transmitting a kilobyte of data really is now too cheap to meter . . . Soon the same will be true for a megabyte, and then soon after a terabyte."[9]

Digital commerce and communications infrastructures have set the stage for business process innovations in many consumer industries today—including health care, retailing, mobile communications, and perhaps industry categories that don't even have names yet! In his first book, *The Concept of the Corporation*, Peter Drucker, the legendary and prolific management thinker, argued for the economic importance of creating community and meeting individuals' social needs.

Ancient mathematics combined with modern computers give companies the best management tools they have ever had to profitably serve needs in society—often, needs that have never been met.

That book was published in 1939, yet seventy years later ancient mathematics, combined with modern computers, gives companies the best management tools they have ever had to profitably serve needs in society—often, needs that have never been met. Indeed, there have never been more exciting new possibilities for corporations to use masses of transaction data to create better business models and more efficient operations that lead to social and economic benefits for everyone.

How Google Rules the Internet by Advertising with Analytics

Google is well known for being able to build a business model around analytics, as there really is no company in the world that surpasses its skills in using math to make money from digital data. Google's founders, Sergey Brin and Larry Page, made their breakthrough in search engine algorithms by meticulously counting and weighting links between and among millions of web pages. Advertising is its biggest revenue source today, but Google is constantly doing R&D to find the next big products and business models.

As we all know, every time a person uses the World Wide Web to shop, to learn, or to relax, he or she creates a data trail that has a story to tell. Any business that has the tools to analyze data from the Internet or other digital channels—and the imagination to piece together the story—has the opportunity to create business value. But as we also know, companies founded in the Internet age are not the only leaders in analytics.

> *Any business that has the tools to analyze data from the Internet or other digital channels—and the imagination to piece together the story—has the opportunity to create business value.*

How Tesco's Analytics Creates Unique Shopping Experiences

Tesco, plc, founded in London in 1919 (the Tesco name was taken in 1924), is now the largest grocery and general merchandise retailer in Great Britain by both global sales and domestic market share, and the fourth largest grocery retailer in the world. The company is also a world leader in the mass retail industry for it application of analytics to create unique and personalized value for individual customers. Dunnhumby, a U.K.-based consulting firm specializing in analytics, has worked with Tesco since 1991 to grow this capability. Dunnhumby created algorithms to run Tesco store operations that analyze and make decisions based on a flow of data and analysis of transactions generated by interactions with *thirteen million* Tesco ClubCard members across *fifty-five thousand product lines*. Tesco now owns a majority share of Dunnhumby, which has also entered into a joint-venture with Kroger, the U.S. supermarket chain.

Years of investments in analytics have enabled Tesco to differentiate its customer experience from competitors'. Although Tesco has not invested in the specific decision management technologies we will discuss later on, it has created a world-class system to make a variety of inventory management and marketing decisions to maximize per customer profitability. Tesco also emphasizes creating value from customer data to make decisions to achieve personalization and convenience for customers that keeps them coming back. (We'll describe Tesco and its ClubCard loyalty program in more detail in the next chapter.)

> Companies in emerging markets are coupling analytics and information technologies to come up with business innovations not yet seen in more economically mature countries.

It's not just international giants that are using analytics successfully. There are plenty of companies in emerging markets investing in decision management technology that are coming up with business innovations not yet seen in more economically mature countries. For example, Akbank, Turkey's largest consumer bank, started developing a banking service using mobile phones as a direct-to-consumer channel in 2006. You may be surprised to find out that in the United States, most money center retail banks didn't begin introducing limited mobile banking features (such as checking your bank balance) until 2007, a year after Akbank did in Turkey! Akbank is using a variety of profit-optimization and risk-management decision models, with other banking products, to promote controlled growth, as the bank seeks profitable relationships among diverse consumers, from the ultra-affluent customer to the rising "mass" affluent to first-time account holders. (Chapter Seven provides a more detailed case study of Akbank.)

Decisions in a Post-Managerial World

Consumers are demanding interactive dialogues at a place and time of their choosing. This requires businesses to make more real-time decisions, and more decisions that personalize every transaction, in ways that are of the highest value to each company's customers and that are most profitable for each particular business. As consumers of all generations become more comfortable with and accustomed to interactive and automated commerce, they are coming to expect convenience, a personal touch, and instant gratification.

> Companies are using analytic models to *automate* decisions or *guide and support* mid-level managers and frontline workers as they manage tasks that affect customer value.

In many cases, there are still competitive and practical implementation issues that prevent large companies from serving a true market of one, but the ability to profitably serve millions of unique customer segments is becoming a reality; moreover, in some industries, it's a competitive necessity. Inside corporations, the silos of autonomous product lines, departments, and geographies are slowly coming down. Making decisions in an environment where functional boundaries are falling and the pressure is on managers to do more with fewer people and tighter budgets demands unprecedented information visibility and coordination at an enterprise level. Coordination and collaboration are *in*; bureaucratic behavior is still prevalent but on its way *out*.

The ability to profitably serve millions of unique customer segments is becoming a reality; moreover, in some industries, it's a competitive necessity.

Strategic plans and competitive responses that used to be analyzed and rolled out episodically over a period of months (or even years) are now happening, in some cases, overnight or in real time—for example, decisions to adjust prices, product features, or the ways in which different customers are treated. And as companies get larger and more complex, it becomes increasingly difficult to translate executive strategy—especially customer strategy—through layers of decision makers, all the way to the frontline people who are closest to the customer. As we pointed out at the beginning of this chapter, Jay Forrester said way back in the 1950s that the modern corporation was too big a social system to manage without computers. Think about that comment in the context of the typical large twenty-first-century company, with two hundred thousand people carrying out millions of decisions every day, based on maybe five decisions made by ten people at the top!

You must enable businesses to make thousands and thousands of individual decisions. . . . but you have to create the infrastructure to make it easy.

Many businesses have spent years squeezing cost savings from automating and outsourcing clerical and basic administrative tasks. Now companies are focusing on more complex decision-making productivity: using decision models and automation to *drive, guide, and support* decisions of mid-level managers and frontline workers as they manage tasks that affect customer value.

In a freewheeling conversation in *The McKinsey Quarterly*, Lowell Bryan, a managing partner at McKinsey, and management guru Gary Hamel discussed the nature of the "post-managerial society" that Hamel describes in his 2008 book, *The Future of Management*. "Increasingly, the work of management won't be done by managers. Instead, it will be pushed out to the periphery. It will be embedded in systems. The idea that you mobilize human labor through a hierarchy of overseers and bureaucrats and administrators is going to look extraordinarily antiquated a decade or two from now," said Hamel.

Bryan responded: "These thinking-intensive people are increasingly self-directed. In fact, they're directed as much by their peers as they are by their supervisors. The management challenge is akin to urban planning. The art of it is that you must enable people to make thousands and thousands of individual decisions. . . . but you have to create the infrastructure to make it easy."[10]

In Chapter Four, we will describe the automation of analytics software that makes this art and science work, as well as Fair Isaac's view of how a decision management infrastructure that automates, improves, and connects decisions is built over time.

Conclusion

The business notions and phrases *decision management* and *competing on analytics* did not exist when Bill Fair and Earl Isaac started the Fair Isaac Corporation. They still called what they were doing *operations research*. Scoring models were one of the first innovations and examples of what Fair Isaac considers to be a decision management tool, although operations research is still thriving and recognized as a profession. Indeed, the Institute for Operations Research and the Management Sciences (INFORMS)—the operations research profession's largest trade association, based in the United States—calls operations research the "science of better" and has even claimed scienceofbetter.org as its URL on the Internet (an idea we wish we had thought of first).

But we do claim decision management as one of operation research's progeny; it is a business discipline growing in influence. Scoring was a disruptive innovation in consumer lending, and adaptive control technology played a critical role in the rapid growth of the credit card industry. Over the next two decades, many new technologies and techniques will emerge in retailing, health care services, insurance, and mobile communications and other transaction-intensive businesses poised for growth and disruptive innovations. Decision management technology, which includes the automation of analytics in operations and the connectivity of decisions, is a critical part of the infrastructure that is making this happen.

But it is important to keep in mind that decision management technology is not, and never has been, intended to completely replace people with computers. Ray Kurzweil, another computer science visionary who got his start at MIT in the 1970s, is a prolific author of futuristic books about artificial intelligence technologies. In his 2006 book *The Singularity Is Near: When Humans Transcend Biology*, he made the prediction that humankind is moving toward a world of technological "singularity," where artificial intelligence in machines exceeds human intelligence.

We prefer the words *synergy* and *symbiosis* rather than *singularity* to discuss the meeting of the minds of human beings and computers in decision management. Decision management models are used to perform computer-based analytics and execute decisions, to modulate human bias and straight-from-the-gut thinking, to improve decisions and results. As we said earlier, the best uses of analytics come from a productive union of brain and computer power. For all the innovations and advantages in life that come from companies becoming more adept and capable of analyzing consumer data and behavior, human judgment and intuition based on expertise and experience is a key element in the success of information-based business strategy and execution.

We will later explain how analytics and decision management go together, but before we get to that, Chapter Two presents several case studies that show how some major companies, in a variety of industries, are successfully using analytics to improve their decision-making processes—which benefits not only their customers but also their bottom line.

2

HOW ANALYTICS MAKES CUSTOMER RELATIONSHIPS MORE VALUABLE

The Experience of Netflix, Best Buy, Tesco, and Harrah's

As we learned in the preceding chapter's history of Fair Isaac and its development of the credit score, predictive analytics is a powerful tool to analyze individual behavior and segments of customers (such as good drivers versus bad drivers) to manage risk and profitability. Analytics is an equally powerful tool you can use to positively affect your customer's experience.

Every company wants to deliver the best experiences at a competitive profit for their industry. But what happens when a customer loves an experience and it is not profitable for the company to provide it? This tension between objectives for financial performance and customer experiences is a constant challenge, especially for mass marketers. The basic premise behind the traditional scale mass-market business models is to maximize profits by relentlessly lowering the cost of producing, selling, and delivering a product or service, or by raising the price to the consumer. Companies rise or fall on their margins, whether this creates a good experience for the customer or not.

Sharper market segmentations and the use of predictive analytics are making it easier for companies to reconcile conflicts between the *push* for profit and the *pull* of positive customer experiences. When you perform analysis, make decisions, and take action based on deep insights about your customers' behavior—generated from billions of your company's customer transactions and interactions—you can be more responsive to individual and group preferences and sensitivities, all the while taking into account your company's specific financial considerations.

Among the client companies we have worked with or observed, the ones that are trying to become customer-centric focus their entire enterprise on these questions:

- Who are our target customers?
- What is the winning sales and service proposition for each customer?
- How does everyone work together to improve the customer experience continuously?
- How does each employee's behavior increase shareholder value and customer loyalty?
- How do we identify and fulfill customers' unspoken needs?

There is a close connection between analytics and customer-centricity.

With that in mind, this chapter offers insights on how leading customer-centric companies are *using* both descriptive (describing customer behavior and traits) and predictive analytics (predicting customer behavior and traits). Some of these companies are clients. Others are organizations we admire and enjoy as consumers. You'll learn

- How Netflix beat Blockbuster in the online DVD and video rental market, *not* by rewarding its customers with old-fashioned price discounting, but by helping them *find more movies* they would enjoy renting, based on what they rented in the past and how they rated those choices.
- How Tesco made online grocery shopping profitable by making it *easy* for customers to buy what they really wanted—by

showing customers their personalized "Favourites List" of food and products they buy regularly, instead of forcing them to wade through the thirty thousand items the store offers.

- How Best Buy analyzed and humanized its different customer types (into suburban moms, gadget guys, and so on) and then tailored its reward program to each type: naturally, suburban moms want something different from what a twenty-something gadget guy wants.

- How Harrah's realized that 82 percent of its revenues came from only 26 percent of its customers—and because those customers weren't high-rolling bigwigs but ordinary middle-class folks, Harrah's moved beyond Atlantic City and Las Vegas to bring gaming centers closer to its best customers and found other unusual ways to reward them for their business.

These companies' experiences will give you great ideas for how you can think about your own customers' preferences differently—and use the information you have about your customers to better advantage, for both them and you. But they will also show that you can get more business value from customer data if you don't try to squeeze the most profit out of every customer transaction. The science of analytics is doing the math to make the business model work. The art is having the empathy and foresight to appreciate and understand how your customers think.

How Netflix Beat Blockbuster—By Tracking What Customers Really Want

The Internet has, of course, been the catalyst for much more than changes in mass marketing. It has inspired entirely new approaches to business competition. Netflix, the U.S.-based movie-rental company, is one of the best examples of a company that disrupted an industry by using the Internet and analytics.

When Reed Hastings founded Netflix in 1999, he saw video stores as a prime target for disruption, and he saw Blockbuster, Inc., then the market leader, as the one to beat. The Blockbuster video store chain dominated the strip malls across America and had put many of the local stores out of business.

Hastings realized that the Internet was an ideal channel to use to grow a customer base fast, and to challenge a major bricks-and-mortar competitor. No driving. Not late fees. Bigger selection. Netflix promoted them all. In addition, Hastings, a former math teacher and computer science grad from Stanford (just like Bill and Earl), realized he could use *predictive analytics* to understand what movies and TV shows people would want to rent and buy. From 1999 to 2006, the company used the Internet to sign up customers and place orders and the postal service to distribute the DVDs. Netflix grew from $5 million to $1.3 billion in 2007.[1] Let's look at the details of how Hastings achieved this dramatic growth.

> Netflix rewards its regular customers by determining what they prefer and giving them more of what they want and more choices.

While Netflix was experiencing phenomenal growth through the Internet, Blockbuster didn't launch its online service until August 2004—five years after Netflix got started. Moreover, Blockbuster hasn't been able to grow its customer base to *even within striking distance* of Netflix: in 2008, Netflix claimed 7.5 million customers, although the company did concede 2.5 million to other DVD rental competitors. Nor has Blockbuster been able to beat its rival on the quality of the experience Netflix has sustained through its mathematical skills and business acumen. In the first half of 2007, Blockbuster used heavy price discounting to "buy" market share from Netflix, but in third-quarter 2007, when Blockbuster raised its prices so it would stop losing money, roughly 15 percent of its customers left.

Where Netflix outshines Blockbuster most is through its recommendation engine, Cinematch. It runs proprietary predictive algorithms that analyze individual customer buying patterns and opinion ratings of movies to predict which movies the person will like. The algorithm is written to optimize both a customer's preferences and inventory conditions. It can also pick up on a customer's tastes for obscure and cult movies. For example, Larry is a member and recently found he had 1,382 suggestions based on 255 ratings. Netflix makes this tally visible, to encourage its customers to rate films and to give them more information about films they might like to see.

So although Blockbuster rewards its regular customers with volume discounts (that is, if you order more movies, you'll pay less for each one), Netflix rewards its regular customers by determining what they prefer and giving them more of what they want, and more choices. In other words, the value is not in rewarding regular purchases but in *capturing information* from every purchase, which builds a *proprietary customer profile* that Blockbuster, Netflix's main competitor, does not have. As the old Fats Waller song goes, "Find out what they want, and how they want it, and give it to 'em just that way."

How Tesco Made Online Grocery Shopping Profitable

In the grocery business, Tesco is another company with analytic skill we admire. Indeed, the U.K.-based multinational grocer has set a new standard for making a customer-centric business model work at scale. For those readers who may be unfamiliar with this company, you'll be interested to know it's the largest retailer in the U.K. (by both global sales and market reach) and *the fourth largest retailer in the world*. Tesco has come a long way from its humble beginnings: in 1919, it was a single stall selling surplus groceries in the East End of London, and Jack Cohen, who opened that stall, brought in only £4 in sales and only £1 in profit on his first day. In 2005 Tesco announced profits of

$2 billion, and the company now sells not only groceries but also nonfood goods as varied as consumer electronics and other home entertainment, clothing, health and beauty products, stationery, cookware, soft furnishings, and seasonal goods (like barbecues and garden furniture).

So how did the company become so successful?

For decades, Tesco had been an undistinguished British grocery frequented by pound-pinching British consumers. Anyone who knew Tesco before the 1990s could never have guessed that it would become the leading grocer in the value-for-price category in the U.K. and, by revenues, the biggest internet grocery service and the third-largest multinational grocery company in the world. When CEO Terry Leahy joined Tesco in 1980, the company had only one computer(!), and it was struggling to shed its legacy image from its founder's slogan, "Pile it high, and sell it cheap."

However, by the mid-1990s the company had made significant investments in warehousing customer data on more than a million of its regular customers and in the analytic tools to learn about and serve individual needs. Those investments made Tesco a strong contender in e-grocery shopping and home delivery. The first movers in this category included Webvan and Peapod, both in the United States, and in the U.K., Marks & Spencer and ASDA (which is now owned by Wal-Mart). Tesco was right up there competing with those innovators, but Tesco was savvy enough to move into territory that its competitors had yet to contemplate.

The Company Clubcard: Tracking Everything You Need to Know About Your Customers. In 1994 Tesco hired Dunnhumby, a small analytics consultancy started by Clive Humby—a trained mathematician and self-described "data-miner extraordinaire"— and his wife and business partner Edwina Dunn. Tesco's senior managers wanted Dunnhumby to help them get more value from the data they were collecting through Tesco's customer loyalty program, Clubcard. The program was launched in February 1995, and the following autumn a Tesco store in West London, which had been the site of a home delivery service trial, took the next step to e-delivery.

At the time, there were not enough people using the Internet at home to support such a service. So to get customers started, Tesco offered them the option to shop on a simple internet site or a CD-ROM–based catalogue supported by a small number of telephone operators. Tesco's Clubcard tracked each member's every transaction and stored it in a large data warehouse. The detailed information on individuals and their grocery shopping grew with every transaction, tracking all of the following:

- The location of the Tesco store they went to most often
- What they bought
- How often they shopped
- Where they lived
- The size of the family
- Even their life stage and lifestyle

> Tesco's Clubcard tracked each member's every transaction and stored it in a large data warehouse.

Once Tesco Direct moved to the Web in 1999, the popularity of the service and the effectiveness of the data collection and analytics took off. For example, the dedicated e-commerce team, now running the web-based service, came up with the idea of posting a customer's "Favourites List" for returning e-shoppers. If you were using the system, instead of it forcing you to wade through a list of thirty thousand items, after your first online order Tesco used your Clubcard data to show you your favorites, based on records of your previous weekly purchases. The website was also starting to offer nongrocery items. The web team created an internet-only customer segmentation model that predicted customer profitability and behavior, and it measured responses to special e-voucher offers. The model reduced the cost of distributing discount coupons, and it raised the response rate among people who bought products every week. Tesco Direct became profitable in 2001 and has stayed in the black ever since.

Webvan, which launched in the United States at the same time, had impressive management credentials and backers, including Louis Borders (who had already made one fortune in the mass retailing of books and at some of the top venture capitalist firms in Silicon Valley). Moreover, Webvan's CEO was George Shaheen, a former head of Accenture. In stark contrast with Tesco, all that Webvan execs knew about their customers was what standard macro market research told them. Webvan's strategy was to attract a critical mass of customers as quickly as possible. They committed most of their start-up funding to build an expensive distribution network to support a twenty-six-city expansion plan.

But Tesco left Webvan in the dust because of Tesco's analysis of customer data. Here's how Clive Humby sums up Tesco's success: "Without Clubcard, the company would have had all the risk and the insurmountable cost of customer acquisition that killed off services like Webvan."[2]

Currently, a member of *one in three households* in the U.K. has signed up for a Clubcard, and each family member has his or her own purchasing profile with data that is added every time that customer shops or responds to a promotion. Every time a Clubcard member swipes a card at the checkout register, the Dunnhumby database collects new data on each item purchased.

Tesco uses its analysis to achieve all of these benefits:

- It finely delineates its customers' shopping patterns and tailors its shopping experiences accordingly.
- It increases the company's profitability.
- It provides the company with a continuous source of information it can use to differentiate the company from competitors.

Tesco's customer loyalty Clubcard could be seen as an analytics equivalent, for the grocery industry, to Netflix's Cinematch for the online rental entertainment industry.

Many stock analysts covering the retail industry have studied and cited different reasons for Tesco's remarkable transformation in the U.K. But the most compelling reason—according to Mike Tattersall, analyst at JPMorgan Cazenove—is Tesco's loyalty card, which has earned the grocer its retail supremacy in Great Britain.[3] It remains to be seen whether Tesco will be successful exporting its analytic system to the United States, the next major market it aims to conquer.

> Tesco gathers so much information that it has been described as "a mind-numbing flow of data on the purchases of 13 million members across 55,000 product lines."

Tesco's Analytics Takes Big Bytes of Customer Information. Tesco's Clubcard program "generates a mind-numbing flow of data on the purchases of 13 million members across 55,000 product lines," says *The Economist*.[4] Models analyzing preferences and behaviors use forty to fifty customer variables from a 40-terabyte database to characterize customers. For example:

- Convenience shoppers are subdivided into narrower categories: *time-poor, food-rich, can't cook, won't cook.* Then analytics can determine how often these people buy prepared meals and the types they buy.

- The system can deduce, from purchasing patterns, if someone is a diabetic; Tesco then sends them offers for sugarless products.

- Mathematical techniques can predict that if a customer is buying certain products—for example, a lot of beef and no breads or pastas—that person is probably on the Atkins diet. Tesco will then refrain from sending offers for high-carb products to these customers. The model can predict how long a person has been on the diet or whether the person's shopping patterns are changing, and this information may be used to project sales of bread and pasta months ahead.

An algorithm called *the rolling ball*, which is updated every year or two, associates customer attributes and preferences with each of the products on Tesco's shelves. For example, the rolling ball might start by giving ratings for specialty items, such as ostrich burgers; it goes on to determine what kinds of specialty and staple items are ending up in the same shopper's basket. Martin Hayward, director of consumer strategy at Dunnhumby, summed it up this way: "All this sophisticated data analysis, and it comes down to where you put the biscuits."[5] But it is rocket science compared with the way grocers used to manage product placement in stores: a decade ago, believe it or not, grocery retailers collected data on customer purchasing behavior by asking customers to fill out questionnaires! In an even more rudimentary approach, they simply counted items on the supermarket shelf, or stores hired a researcher to walk around the store recording a selection of customers' purchases.

Best Buy Sharpens Its Customer Focus

Like Tesco, Best Buy, Inc., is a retailer zeroing in on what its customers want by focusing on the point of purchase. Since 2001 Best Buy has been developing a foundation of customer data and analytics to support standardized business processes that create nuanced, varied, and personalized experiences for its customers.

Best Buy is the largest consumer electronics retailer in North America, with $40 billion in annual revenue. And the company expects to grow still further: at the company's annual shareholders' meeting in June 2008, Best Buy's chief operating officer Brian Dunn declared plans to double the company's sales to $80 billion by 2013.

The company has come a long way from its humble beginnings in 1966, when it was a single stereo store called the Sound of Music in St. Paul, Minnesota. In 1989, the name was changed to Best Buy as the successful statewide chain launched its big push to become a leading national player. Over the next ten years, the company opened hundreds of superstores in rapid succession in shopping centers throughout the United States.

Outside, Best Buy's big, boldly colored blue-and-yellow stores stood out. Inside, selections of popular televisions, cameras, printers, PCs, music and videos, and all the accessories, plus home appliances—washers and dryers, refrigerators and ranges—filled the then-novel warehouse-style space that became known as "big box" retailing. The company originally dubbed its retail format "grab and go."

Changing the Focus on Products to a Focus on Customers. During the 1990s, Best Buy seemed invincible, in many ways:

- While several regional chains faltered, Best Buy's growth never wavered.
- It grew annual revenues at a 25-percent annual clip by opening stores and adding new customers across the United States.
- Earnings per share grew faster than Microsoft's, and its shareholder returns beat Intel's.[6]
- In 1996 Best Buy surpassed its main national rival, Circuit City, in revenues and market share, to become the leading consumer electronics retailer in the United States.

From its beginnings in Minnesota, Best Buy's growth strategy had always been to deliver markedly better customer experiences than its competitors. And the company was still doing well by being customer-focused when, in 2002, CEO Brad Anderson decided Best Buy needed to take its value proposition for the customer to a new level. As he sized up the situation, he knew the company could not sustain the roughly 25-percent growth per year that Wall Street had come to expect, just by opening new stores and by acquiring new customers. As Tesco had done in the grocery business, Best Buy would focus on *delivering outstanding customer experiences* in the consumer electronics and appliance category: this focus would become the company's ultimate driver of growth, differentiation, and profits.

Anderson proposed a multiyear, multi-million-dollar plan to change the company's traditional *product-centric* scale retail model to a mass *customer-centric* approach. Best Buy's leadership took on customer-centricity as an enterprise-wide strategy:

- Changing roles and responsibilities of executives and managers
- Using sophisticated customer segmentations to redesign individual stores tailored in a single store for multiple customer segments
- Training and learning about the segmentations for all employees—especially store personnel, known as the Blue Shirts

Anderson's management team and Wall Street were nervous at the time that this might be too big an undertaking, but he assured them that, in the long run, investments in building analytic capabilities, store reformatting, and training were essential to the strategy of profitably serving the needs of customers one store at a time, and building loyalty one customer at a time, throughout the chain.

"Much like personal relationships, we think that the tone of the customer dialogue changes as that relationship gets deeper, more familiar, and intimate. Our challenge is to convey to tens of millions of customers with hundreds of millions of transactions a year, very personal messages that represent our effort to deepen the relationship with them." So Matt Smith, Best Buy's senior director of customer insight, told us in an interview in 2007.

Smith, who joined the company in 2004, is part of a team that has led Best Buy's work with analytics. Today, he oversees web analytics, one-to-one marketing, the Reward Zone customer-loyalty program, market-share measurement, in-store test-and-measurement, and an analytics R&D team that serves multiple operating groups. (Learn more about the Reward Zone program later in this chapter.)

Step 1: Analyzing Customers' Purchasing Behavior and Assessing Which Customers Are Most Valuable. In 2002, the first step was to analyze existing customers' purchasing behaviors and predict which ones could be the most profitable relationships. A proprietary customer value model, developed by the Customer Insight group, measured customer profitability performance along two dimensions:

1. Share of wallet
2. Forecasted future lifetime customer value, based on purchase histories

For example, if a customer buys a lot of low-margin products and comes into the store only infrequently, the model doesn't forecast a high lifetime value for that customer.

The proprietary customer value model also categorized Best Buy customers in five segments:

> *The proprietary customer value model characterized Best Buy customers in five segments: new, uncommitted, lapsed, "opportunity," and best customers.*

1. *New* customers
2. *Uncommitted* customers
3. *Lapsed* customers
4. *Opportunity* customers
5. *Best* customers

Best Buy needed to win over thirty-nine "uncommitted" customers to recoup the lifetime value of losing just one of its "best" customers.

Turning just 5 percent more people into "opportunity" customers would yield $1 billion in revenues.

An "opportunity" customer might be someone who comes in every sixty days to buy printer accessories and could end up buying other high-margin products as well.

The model also clearly showed that Best Buy needed to win over thirty-nine uncommitted customers to recoup the lifetime value of losing just one of its best customers. At that time, uncommitteds were 12 percent of its customer base. The model also showed that turning just 5 percent more people into opportunity customers would yield $1 billion in revenues.

Step 2: *Humanizing Customer Segments.* The next phase was to put a human face on these segments. Using a mix of demographic, behavioral, and attitudinal segmentations, plus some macroeconomic analysis woven in, the following characterizations of customers emerged, and the company gave names to each type of buyer:

- "Barry" is an affluent technology enthusiast.
- "Jill" is a busy young suburban mother.
- "Ray" is a price-conscious family man.
- "Buzz" is a young gadget fiend.

These personas were used to redesign the format of a select group of stores that were chosen as laboratories for applying customer insights and segmentations. Each "lab" store experimented with different formats, product assortments, and sales and service engagement models—even the lighting. Most stores were changed to address just one persona segment (although some experimented with multiple personalities).

Lab store performance was closely measured as Best Buy tested, experimented, refined, and prepared for a broader rollout of segment stores. By 2005, the new segment concepts had been tested in thirty-five stores.

Best Buy's Blue Shirts received extensive training to familiarize themselves with the different segments and were coached on different ways to relate to them. Specialized salespeople, such as personal sales assistants for "Jill" and home-theater experts for "Buzz" and "Barry," get additional training that may last weeks.

"Our analytics is translated into something our sales associates understand and use to engage customers," says Smith. For example, in conversations with customers, salespeople are trained to filter through a series of lifestyle questions informed by the analytics, such as:

"How are you going to use this product?"

"Are you buying this digital camera for yourself or someone else?"

In the home appliance area, if someone is shopping for a washing machine and dryer, a salesperson might ask:

"What type of clothes are you cleaning and drying?"

"Do you have space constraints?"

The questions are designed to get to know more about the customer's needs, rather than to close a sale, and to further enrich the analytic database.

Best Buy's leaders of the merchandising function (known in the company as "the merchant groups") are among the most powerful executives in the company. The impact of the segmentation work on these teams has been significant. Instead of

managers in the merchant groups interacting with manufacturers along product lines, the different merchant teams are now
split into the following categories:

- An entertainment group
- A mobility group (for products used on the move, such as
  cell phones, laptops, digital phones, and digital cameras)
- A home group for bundles of products such as home theaters
  and appliances.

Now when buyers talk to Kodak, they ask about the photo
printer, the camera, and the memory card together in one conversation, rather than just asking about camera assortments.
Selling the cameras is important, but selling the printer and
memory card is too.

*Using analytics to learn
about its customers, Best
Buy doubled its sales from
$20 billion to $40 billion
between 2003 and 2008.*

The merchant groups are also
thinking about differentiated value
propositions for segments. For
example, digital downloading is a
new challenge for Best Buy's entertainment group. They are thinking
about what to do about all pack-
aged media products that still take up a lot of real estate in the
middle of stores, so they're mulling questions like these:

- How many customers are consuming media entirely online?
- How many customers are experientialists who still want to
  hold a DVD or CD and read the playlist on the back before
  they buy?
- What are the implications for store inventory and layouts
  and product promotions strategies?

By 2005, Best Buy was identifying about 40 percent of its
transactions and 50 percent of its revenue using demographic

and behavioral segmentations. For example, one analysis of Buzz's "purchase path" for MP3 players, using historical data from 2003 and 2004, showed that Buzz buys accessories for his MP3 player thirty days after he buys the player itself. He is also five times more likely to buy a digital camera than he is to buy any other product.

Best Buy has come a long way in its journey to customer-centricity, and it continues to work on the strategy store by store. CEO Brad Anderson claims that reformatted stores have doubled their growth rate compared with stores that have yet to be transformed. And the company doubled its overall sales from $20 billion to $40 billion between 2003 and 2008.

Our own visit to Best Buy's flagship store in Richfield, Minnesota, a stone's throw from the corporate headquarters, revealed noticeable improvements. The computer section had clearly marked areas for small business computing, a section for Apple products and accessories, and a section for several brands of multimedia PCs. In the PC area there were clusters of products for video and photo cataloging and editing, with a clear line of sight to digital cameras. This section had amateur photos—shot by Best Buy staff—in frames, showcasing different cameras with different resolutions printed on different printers. Also in the line of sight were external monitors and software for photo editing (such as Adobe Photoshop). We suspect that analytics guided decisions to place products in particular spots to increase traffic to other departments. It also made it easier to navigate around the store and easier for well-prepared Blue Shirts to dig into our application needs.

Best Buy and Tesco both use loyalty cards to continuously gather more data they can use to analyze their customers' behavior. But as we shall read next, customer loyalty program data has historically been underutilized. Even Best Buy and Harrah's, both analytic leaders and leaders in their respective markets, have first made mistakes to figure out how to apply loyalty program data to improving the customer experience.

Developing Customer Loyalty Programs with Relevance

Back in 1981, American Airlines CEO Robert Crandall pioneered the idea in the airline industry that "all fares and customers are not created equal." That comment led to the creation of American Airlines Advantage, the first frequent-flier rewards program. This program was a simple segmentation of customer data from the airline's reservation systems, differentiating three tiers of frequent fliers (silver, gold, and platinum). The most profitable customers got special privileges such as separate check-in and priority upgrades. All members earned miles, based on frequency of travel and dollars spent.

Within a few years, miles became a currency as the model spread throughout the industry. For decades, the "frequent-customer, points for purchase" model had been used for most loyalty programs. This was—and remains, in many industries—a big missed opportunity to use a rich source of data that customers willingly provide, to analyze their behavior. After all, these schemes are a contract: a company agrees to give its regular customers something of value in return for the information that the customers permit the company to know about them. For years, companies missed the chance to use the data as something more than a medium for the exchange of goods and services.

What's important here is not just *collecting* the data but *using* it to learn more about customers. Clive Humby of Dunnhumby, the consultants who worked with Tesco, confirms this key point: "Anyone can launch a points system, but points are just electronic sales promotion. It is just a different way of getting money off [the listed price]. It only becomes a loyalty mechanic when you use the data to add relevance to a customer's life."[7]

This is the approach that Harrah's has adopted, after also making a significant commitment to competing by using analytics to differentiate the Harrah's experience from all other players in the industry and to go after valuable customer segments that competitors did not care about or did not see.

Harrah's Learns How to Use Customer Reward Data

Harrah's is the largest gaming company in the world, with revenues in 2007 of $7.11 billion. Harrah's CEO Gary Loveman, a former Harvard business school professor, left the business school in 1998 to become the company's COO. He is well known for being a champion of Harrah's competencies in analytics. Harrah's pursued geographic diversification in the late 1990s, under the leadership of Loveman's predecessor, Phil Satre. Eschewing the billion-dollar investments its competitors made in the large and lavish facilities in America's gambling meccas of Atlantic City and Las Vegas, Satre chose to make casino gambling a *local* entertainment option for gambling enthusiasts and to bring the Harrah's experience to them.

It was during this period of expansion that Harrah's discovered, through analytics, that its best customers were not, as Loveman put it, "the gold-cufflinked, limousine-riding high rollers"[8] that all casino operators traditionally court. In fact, they were middle-aged, middle-class Americans—teachers,

> *Harrah's customer analytics is the core of its business model, and its competency is unmatched in the industry: one hundred people manage and mine that customer database.*

doctors, and machinists—who enjoyed playing the slot machines. Although these customers generated 82 percent of its revenues, analysis showed they represented only 26 percent of the customer base. Obviously, if the company could increase this customer base, its revenues would soar as well. So in 1997, Harrah's launched a customer loyalty program called Total Gold, which followed the frequent-flier model. Before a customer began his session, he inserted his Total Gold card into the slot machine, and he earned credits as he pulled the lever. Points were redeemed for dinners, hotel rooms, show tickets, and gift certificates.

Although there were some initial problems, the company quickly recognized the value in the data being collected. "By tracking millions of individual transactions, the information-technology systems that underlie the program had assembled a vast amount of data on customer preferences," said Loveman.[9] At the core of the program was a 300-gigabyte transactional database that recorded customer activity at various points-of-sale—slot machines, restaurants, and other retail areas on the properties. Today, Harrah's customer analytics is the core of its business model, and its competency is unmatched in the industry: the company has created a Customer Insight Team: *one hundred people* who manage and mine that customer database.

Behavior-based segmentations might slice and dice data in demographic groups and income to find big spenders in unexpected places. For example, Harrah's analysts can identify the elderly middle-income customer who enjoys the shows and the slot machines, and may be more profitable than the wealthier retiree who has more to spend but skips the entertainment. Harrah's captures data on individual and group behaviors and spending patterns in single and multiple locations. Are they starting to wander away from the slots to the blackjack tables? How much are they spending on each activity? Harrah's knows this.

And the company *uses* its customer database across the organization for big and small marketing decisions: what channels to use for what customer type and which messages to craft for different channels. Here are just a few examples:

- When a customer who usually spends $1,000 a month has not visited her local casino in three months, the database triggers a letter or a phone call to invite her back.

- Customized marketing promotions encourage regular customers to choose different Harrah's casinos when they travel in the United States. The database enables the company to communicate to individuals directly with customized or personalized messages.

- Specific properties use the database to do "marketing interventions" when guests are in the casinos. An intervention might be vouchers for food and entertainment to keep them in the casino longer.

Total Reward (formerly Total Gold) members still earn points for activity, but their rewards are tailored based on personal transactions. The power of the database is being able to track and direct millions of peripheral offers that please individuals and keep them coming back. The Customer Insight Team tracks 80 percent of its revenue through the Total Rewards program, according to Forrester Research. "While it is difficult to extrapolate the precise value of the customer rewards program, it certainly has been a key driver of the company's overall success," says Forrester analyst David Frankland.[10]

How Best Buy's Improved "Reward Zone" Tripled the Membership

Harrah's isn't the only company, of course, that is learning how to use its customer information more effectively. Even Best Buy, with its full corporate press to become customer-centric, didn't initially realize it was underutilizing its Reward Zone customer loyalty program when it was first launched in 2004, according to Best Buy's VP of customer insight Matt Smith. Customers paid a $9.95 fee to become a member, and they received points and certificates they could use for future store purchases. For the company's in-store Blue Shirts, Reward Zone was a sale-closing tool for big-ticket items: the logic was that a customer buying a $3,000 TV could easily be convinced to pay $10 for Reward Zone if he knew he'd get $60 worth of certificates to use on his next shopping trip.

The program grew to a respectable eight million members between 2004 and October 2007, when Best Buy relaunched Reward Zone. This time there was no membership fee, and the company made other changes to strengthen the customer relationship-building component of the program. Matt Smith said that, in hindsight, "We realized it was a bit disingenuous to ask a customer to be our best friend for $10. That's not the way we want to build the relationship." Now, he says, "we make it clear to customers the types of behavior that we're rewarding. This could be frequency of spending, longevity, or both." The new Reward Zone was also launched in conjunction with a pilot cobranded Best Buy MasterCard they were trying to scale nationally. By December 2007, there were *twenty-seven million* Reward Zone members—more than triple the original eight million—and Best Buy was adding *1.2 million more members each month.*

We realized it was a bit disingenuous to ask a customer to be our best friend for $10. That's not the way we want to build the relationship . . .

The program retains a "points for purchase" component, but a bigger value for Best Buy is the models that the Customer Insight group has created to analyze Reward Zone transactions and dialogue data. This data is highly valuable for developing special benefits and programs for the best and most profitable customers. For example, in November 2007, Best Buy used the Reward Zone card to offer a preholiday private shopping event to its best customers. It ran six events on a Sunday night, covering 150 stores in 70 markets. Those stores were closed for everybody except customers who received invitations, and at some stores, there were *lines of up to two hundred people* waiting for their turn to go in!

Best Buy spent almost a year restructuring Reward Zone, and it continues to evolve. The sign-up package for Reward Zone encourages new members to create an online account, where they can fill out as much—or as little—information about themselves as they choose. "If you give your birth date, you get a special offer on your birthday," says Smith. Best Buy also sends articles and insights from the tech press, such as CNET, to "Barry" customers (the affluent technology enthusiasts) and to "multichannel techsperts." And in 2007, Best Buy sponsored The Police tour and gave some of its best customers the opportunity to sing with Sting during sound checks. *That's* a cool reward!

New ideas for Reward Zone are discussed all the time. The next special services for premier-tier customers might focus on taking stress out of the buying experience. (The analogy is first-class treatment on an airplane.) Another option is free data backup delivered by Geek Squad, the company's tech support service. When a computer bought at Best Buy crashes, it's protected on a Best Buy server. If you want Deal of the Day information from the stores that are closest to you, Best Buy could give you the ability to ask for this information through an RSS message feed or SMS text message, and Best Buy could respond instantaneously. "We couldn't afford to do these things for everybody because it breaks the business model. But we can do it for some," says Smith.

Conclusion

In their book *Competing for the Future: Co-Creating Unique Value with Customers*, C. K. Prahalad and Venkat Ramaswamy use a simple chart that juxtaposes sets of words that influence how managers think and how customers think, as shown in Figure 2.1. Whereas managers think about call centers, logistics, and, technology platforms, customers (including us, when we are not at work) think about what makes us happy, what's convenient, what our kids want for their birthdays, and what we want for ourselves.

In our work we try to think both ways, and as consumers and business people we think the quality of communications and understanding between companies and customers is improving as more information is exchanged by both parties. Customer and company concerns will always differ, but at the point of interaction, consumer thinking and company thinking can come closer together through the use of math and analytics.

Think about it. Analytics that describe and predict consumer behavior increase managerial awareness of what consumers are doing and thinking. As we will show in the next chapter, more and more companies are not just collecting digital information

Figure 2.1 Company Think versus Consumer Think

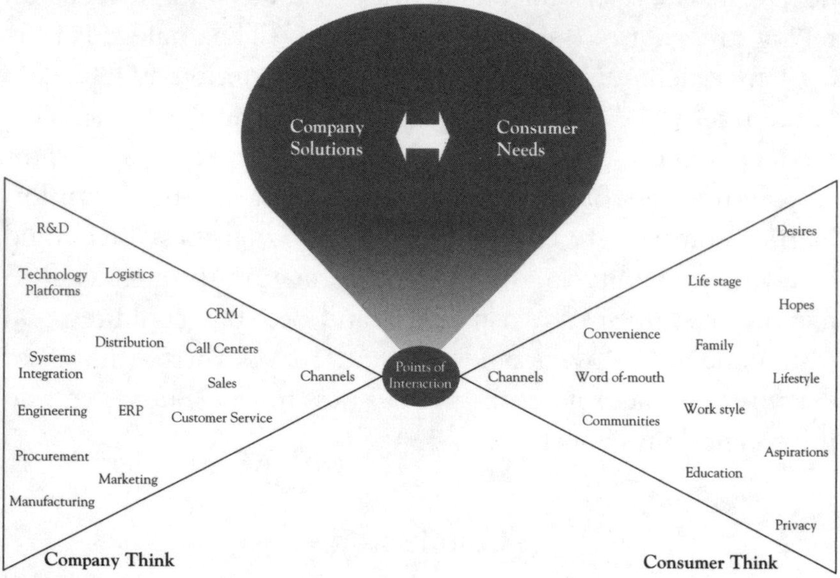

Company Solutions ⬌ Consumer Needs

R&D

Technology Platforms   Logistics

CRM

Systems Integration   Distribution   Call Centers

Sales

Engineering   ERP   Customer Service

Procurement

Marketing

Manufacturing

Channels   Points of Interaction   Channels

Convenience

Word of-mouth

Communities

Desires

Life stage

Hopes

Family

Lifestyle

Work style

Aspirations

Education

Privacy

Company Think   **Consumer Think**

Source: Adapted by permission of Harvard Business School Press. *The Future of Competition: Co-Creating Value with Customers* by C. K. Prahalad and Venkat Ramaswamy (2004), 39. Copyright © 2004 by the Harvard Business School Publishing Corp., all rights reserved.

about consumers, but also using digital technology to exchange information and ideas with customers and invite customers to participate directly in the business processes in which managerial decisions are made.

3

CO-CREATION AND DECISION MANAGEMENT

How Consumers and Companies Share Data to Create Value

It's popular these days to say that customers are in control; that companies are no longer the dominant party in the customer relationship. But this is not the same kind of control that mass-producers and marketers have exercised since Henry Ford reputedly told Model-T customers they could have any car they wanted as long as it was black.

Digital commerce is propelling a healthy democratization of the company-customer relationship. Data available to companies and consumers enables both sides to know more about what the other is thinking and doing, and this is creating new opportunities for businesses to create new types of value for consumers and new sources of profit.

In a digital world, public use of private data is here to stay and is going to continue growing. This has people both excited and worried. The excitement comes from innovations such as interactive online communities, in which consumers can bond with their favorite brands; personalized treatment of diseases; and more marketing news that consumers can use. The worry is privacy. Can consumers trust companies with their data? How secure is the data? What is a fair exchange of data for value between consumers and companies? In this chapter, we look at the changing company-consumer relationship from both sides—the upside of more open and collaborative exchanges of information and communication between companies and consumers, and the challenges of companies getting closer to their customers. To illustrate these challenges, we'll draw on a myriad of companies, including Nike, Coca-Cola, Capital One, Bank of Montreal, insurance companies and finance companies, Facebook, and our own company with its FICO® score.

Always On, Consumer-Centered Marketing

In his book, *Always On: Advertising, Marketing, and Media in an Era of Consumer Control*, Booz & Co. consultant Chris Vollmer says consumers are in control because they have access to more information and more personal and interactive media, such as the Internet, iPods, mobile phones, and other devices that are eclipsing the traditional persuasion media of TV, radio, and print. At the same time, companies have more ways to win consumer attention and stimulate interest.

It doesn't matter how many people are watching; what counts is whether they're paying attention and responding. With knowledge of this kind, marketing is being reborn as a consumer-centered craft.

Indeed, hidden persuasion is more pervasive than ever. A person living in a major American city is exposed to five thousand advertising messages, on average, per day. That's three thousand more ads per person than in the 1970s, according to estimates by the market research firm the Daniel Yankelovich Group.[1] In addition to using new digital media and movie theaters, consumer marketers are using everything from the handles of grocery carts to motion sickness bags on airplanes to expose people to brand images and traits.

"As with the Internet that helped to shape it," Vollmer writes, the new environment is also 'always on' because the consumer is always present: constantly seeking opportunities and value, taking advantage of the multiplying media around it, and (at the same time) being bombarded with ever more media in ever more forms." Because of this, *marketers* must be working constantly to know how consumers are being influenced by advertising and marketing in multiple media, and, more important, how they respond. "It doesn't matter how many people are watching; what counts is whether they're paying attention and responding. With knowledge of this kind, marketing is being reborn as a consumer-centered craft," says Vollmer.[2]

How Nike Practices Always-On Marketing

Two of the world's best-known global brands, Nike and Coca-Cola, are on the leading edge of using the Internet to create always-on marketing experiences that engage individual consumers with the brand. Here are just a few examples of what Nike has done:

- In advance of the 2006 World Cup tournament, Nike partnered with Google to launch an online social community targeting soccer fans and athletes.
- Nike+, a joint venture between Nike and Apple, turned the iPod into a tool for runners to monitor their running performance; using a sensor in their Nike footwear, they track their calorie-burning and heart rates in real time and online.
- At the website NikePlus.com, consumers can post their times, share favorite running routes, compare their performance to that of professional athletes such as Lance Armstrong and LeBron James, and download their favorite motivational music mixes.

Although we don't know exactly how Nike used consumer data and analytics in these marketing programs, we are sure that the company does use these. And we have first hand-knowledge of how Coca-Cola built a decision management system, using Fair Isaac technology, that supports an interactive multibrand marketing program called *MyCoke Rewards*.

How Coca-Cola Practices Precision Engagement

In 2002, a team of marketing executives met at The Coca-Cola Company's Atlanta headquarters to chart the future of the company's brand in a changing competitive environment and an uncharted interactive media environment.

For years, Coca-Cola has been number one on the annual Interbrand Survey, a list of the top one hundred brands in the world. In comparison, in 2007, Pepsi was number twenty-six. The rivalry between these two brands has been known as the Cola Wars.

Today, it's the Beverage Wars, because although there are still die-hard cola fans, cola consumption and market share worldwide has been declining, as beverage choices proliferate. Brand extensions, such as Coke Zero or Pepsi Lemon, help; nevertheless, both Coca-Cola and Pepsi have diversified into health drinks, water, and energy boosters, among others. Between October 2004 and 2007, Coca-Cola launched *thirty different new beverage products* among multiple brands. And in 2007 Coca-Cola made the largest acquisition in its history: a $4.1 billion purchase of Energy Brands, Inc., the maker of Glaceau Vitaminwater.

Meanwhile, in the changing advertising and marketing environment, Coca-Cola's challenge was to figure out how to build a vehicle that could effectively increase consumer mind share and brand loyalty—and ultimately increase consumption of its beverages—on an ongoing basis, one person at a time. In the past, Coca-Cola's marketing was the typical product-by-product approach. In contrast, the new approach coordinates marketing of the entire portfolio of products sold worldwide by the beverage behemoth. In 2004, Coca-Cola invested in a decision management technology platform that serves as the foundation for all the company's interactive marketing programs, across all thirteen brands within the Coca-Cola product portfolio, and on a global scale.

The personalization comes with the MyCoke Rewards brand-loyalty building program. It works like this: After you register for your MyCoke account on the Web, you enter codes that become points in your account. Codes come from inside the bottle tops of beverages you drink. The more time you spend on the site and redeem points, the more precisely Coca-Cola can know what your interests are—and can therefore emotionally engage you. The site captures psychographic information such as music and sports preferences, which, unlike traditional demographic data (such as age and residence) reveals more about *your* individual tastes (no pun intended!) and behavior.[3]

The loyalty program mode is still a points-for-purchase model, but the key is *making the rewards as relevant as possible* to Coca-Cola's prized youth demographic globally (ages thirteen to twenty-five). The experience on the site includes the kinds of content creating, sharing, and communication young people flock to on popular social networking websites.

Launched in 2006, the MyCoke Rewards website includes cutting-edge data collection, analytics, and automated decision management. Here are just a few examples of the rewards target consumers can earn that are tailored to their interests:

- Live music lovers who drink enough Coke can cash in a few thousand reward points to attend a live taping and go backstage at a concert.
- Skiers can escape to a mountain resort for three days.
- NASCAR enthusiasts can win lug nuts from race cars used in NASCAR events.

Although the financial impact of the program—a multiyear effort—is not public, this interactive platform is the first marketing program ever to go across Coca-Cola's thirteen brands, and it is a great example of the power of connecting decisions. Now Coca-Cola can combine actions to maximize the value of a portfolio of brands per customer segment, instead of simply managing a single product, brand by brand. Coca-Cola views all of its interactive marketing efforts as a way to achieve improved marketing efficiency in a fragmented media environment, ultimately reducing the company's traditional reliance on broad-based television advertising promotions.

Companies tend to start from scratch with every new marketing campaign, essentially ignoring the fact that they have already established a relationship with loyalty program members.

Large consumer-branded companies like Coca-Cola have long struggled with how to *get more value* from the databases of people who register for their loyalty programs and have therefore agreed to let companies use their personal information for marketing purposes. Companies tend to start from scratch with every new marketing campaign, essentially ignoring the fact that they have already established a relationship with loyalty program members.

It is relatively easy for companies to populate a consumer database with people's names, addresses, demographic data, and, in some cases, their buying patterns. The bigger challenge, however, is figuring out how to *use* that data to deliver marketing content that is useful and relevant and entertaining to millions of people—one person at a time.

Promotions and brand managers define the rules that describe the marketing strategies that determine which consumers see which content. Then the business rules software takes over, automating the decisions that trigger one text message delivered to a mobile phone, an e-mail, an internet pop-up ad in Beijing, Ankara, New York, Denver. The technology dictates the nature, the pattern, and the sequence of marketing messages to individuals. These can change as the person's consumer data profile changes. A dynamic survey engine captures relevant pieces of data through various iterations of the algorithm. Each decision is based on millions of consumer profiles developed from data collected from multiple customer touch points and stored in a single data warehouse.

Co-Creation in a Digital Marketplace

A few years ago, C. K. Prahalad and Venkat Ramaswamy coined the term *co-creation* to describe how customers become active participants in creating business value with companies that they value, too. The *recommendation engine* is a simple example of data-driven co-creation. As we described in Chapter Two, this is how Netflix beat Blockbuster—by providing recommendations of other movies or TV shows that its customers might want to rent, based on information Netflix customers provided willingly to Netflix, in the form of ratings of the movies they had rented and watched. Of course, Netflix is not the only company doing this, by any means: Amazon, Apple's iTunes, digital music delivery start-ups such as We7 and The Filter.com, and many other sites on the Web are all companies whose regular customers willingly let them analyze their purchasing data. But it takes more than customers giving permission for the data to be analyzed. The more consumers use the services and the recommendation tools on the sites, the better the algorithms get, and the more personalized and appealing the experience becomes over time.

> The more consumers use the services and the recommendation tools on the sites, the better the algorithms get, and the more personalized and appealing the experience becomes over time.

Capital One and Bank of Montreal: Co-Creating Credit Cards with Customers

In the credit card industry today, retail bank issuers, such as Capital One and Bank of Montreal, are using the Internet to let prospective customers "build their own credit card" product. The data exchange makes the cards more attractive to the customer and more profitable for the issuers.

For example, Bank of Montreal's MasterCard card, called Mosaik, is aimed at frequent travelers. Direct marketing campaigns entice prospective customers to visit a website where they can choose their card's primary features, which include five options to earn air miles or cash-back rewards for card usage and two interest rate plans. If they choose the lower interest rate, they pay an annual fee, whereas the higher-rate plan has no fee. Customers can also choose from a selection of optional travel services (all for an annual fee), including trip cancellation insurance, medical protection on long and short trips, and twenty-four-hour travel "concierge services." Mosaik is tribranded in partnership with the Canadian airline WestJet and a third-party data aggregator, Loyalty Management Group of Canada, which designs and operates reward programs. Since the card was launched in 2002, the data shared among the corporate partners has mainly been used to improve targeting and response rates for the direct marketing campaigns.

Capital One, which was an early leader in using data to personalize credit cards, recently launched Card Lab, a more sophisticated application of credit card co-creation. The idea is to encourage individual consumers to select combinations of product features by choosing directly rather than have Capital One infer good combinations of product features by using the individual's data. Like the website for the Mosaik card, Capital One's Card Lab website allows a consumer to select among rewards, interest rates, and fee combinations. As the consumer makes certain choices, other choices are eliminated. For example, if a person checks a box with high rewards and no fee, then the boxes for low APRs are made inactive. If the consumer first selects a rock-bottom APR, then that person cannot choose any of the rewards options.

It's safe to predict that consumer-direct co-creation, through the Web and not just by banks, will grow in different ways. The principle is for *you*, the provider, to figure out what combinations of product or service features best serve *your* interests, and then let your prospect or customer select from those combinations in a manner that best serves his or her needs. Who's in charge of the product feature decisions? Both the customer and the company.

Insurance Companies Try to Use Customer Data—But Face Privacy Issues

Even more complex business models are emerging in automobile and health insurance. Multiple players in these industry value chains are sharing data and co-creating value. For example, a behavior-based "pay as you drive" (PAYD) model sets the insured's premium by monitoring his or her ongoing driving performance with a GPS system installed in the car. Because the cost of the insurance is adjusted dynamically based on behavior, drivers who choose this type of insurance program have an incentive to be careful. Insurance companies in the United States, Great Britain, Australia, Japan, Canada, and South Africa have tried the model.

> The decision-making process becomes even more complex when multiple businesses are involved at the point of interaction to complete a transaction with a consumer.

Suppose the health-insurance premiums paid by a customer with diabetes could be reset continually based on monitoring of that person's vital signs and compliance with a regimen of diet, exercise, and medication. In theory, that model is possible today, and an early version is being tried by ICICI Prudential Life Insurance Company, a joint venture between ICICI, an Indian retail bank, and Prudential plc, an international retail financial services group based in the United Kingdom. (See more about ICICI in Chapter Seven.) The personalized service and the pricing are continually co-created by the customer, the customer's doctor, and ICICI Prudential. The insurance company is also the organizer of a network supporting the program that includes health clubs, pharmaceutical companies specializing in diabetes medication, and diagnostic and testing firms. Patients regularly go to diagnostic clinics for testing the state of their health. The results are used to set the premiums.

Neither of these models is without complications or critics. Norwich Union, Britain's largest insurer, launched its PAYD program in 2006, but the product was discontinued in 2007 because of weak demand. Norwich Union blamed automakers for not supporting installation of the boxes in cars. Also, drivers were put off by the idea of being constantly tracked by a satellite. Questions were raised over invasion of privacy and the use of the data generated from monitoring the movements of a registered vehicle.[4]

A contributor to the Age of Innovation's Blog offers this commentary on the possibility of an insurance product like the one ICICI Prudential offers to diabetics in India being offered in the United States:

> If this kind of program would have a chance of flying in the U.S., providers would have to guarantee an iron-clad lock on the data, both in transit from customer to service provider and stored by the provider. The more paranoid among us can imagine "Do Not Insure" lists making the rounds, or insured diabetics getting harassed by every imaginable marketer in the diabetes-care industry . . . Mistakes in reporting and diagnosis are inevitable, as are security lapses. Are insurance and health care industries really up to this challenge? As a lifelong diabetic myself, this level of monitoring isn't for me—but then again, I eschew modern insulin pumps for the old stick-a-needle-in-my-leg method.

Startup Auto Finance Company Customizes Car Loans for Individual Customers

The decision-making process becomes even more complex when multiple businesses are involved at the point of interaction to complete a transaction with a consumer. For example, consider an automotive purchase in which a car dealer has only ten or fifteen minutes to solicit bids for a financing package from an independent auto lending company to have one ready to present to the potential customers when they return from the test drive of the car they may purchase. The process today is inflexible and labor intensive: dealers request bids from multiple lenders, and lenders present a single fixed offer to the dealer. The dealer picks an offer, but it usually has to negotiate to make the lender's proposed terms fit its needs.

A startup independent auto finance company that we have worked with has created a way to present an offer with a set of variables that the dealer can select and customize to each specific consumer. These variables include duration of the loan, interest rate, purchase price, and down payment amount. By doing this, this approach gives the dealer the authority to make an adjustment to a proposed loan structure without having to consult with the lender. Analytics play a critical role in determining a set of choices for the dealer so that the lender is indifferent about the final financing package the dealer chooses. This business model means the dealer can negotiate unilaterally with the consumer, without having the lender involved. Therefore, dealers have more control over the financing decisions and leeway to give individual customers more one-to-one attention than is the norm in consumer auto financing.

This startup is creating its business from the ground up to be centered on analytics and decision management. In this regard, it is doing for auto finance what Capital One did for the credit card market. Their business design incorporates analytics at each stage of the business process, using segmentation models, predictive models, optimization, and rules engines for tasks like setting loan rates, approving loans, and prioritizing collections. It also designed the business to begin collecting data and experimenting to learn from day one, with the goal of improving the analytics over time. All of this effort is defining a new set of decisions that ripple through from auto finance companies to dealers, from dealers to consumers, and eventually back to the auto finance company.

Credit Consumers Take Control with MyFICO

Consumers are not always aware of the value that can be created for them, because companies don't effectively explain what they are doing. When companies are transparent, the consumer is more educated and confident. Our own experiences with the FICO score support this.

Before Fair Isaac launched the Internet site www.myFICO. com in 2001, many people didn't even know they had a FICO score, unless they happened to read articles that made scoring sound like Big Brother or deliberate discrimination—neither of which is true. Consumer financial literacy and understanding of the FICO score among Americans are still not where we would like them to be, but the situation is getting better.

The FICO score helps bankers make better lending decisions; myFICO helps consumers make better personal finance decisions that improve their credit health.

One purpose of myFICO® is to demystify the FICO score for current or prospective consumers of credit products, but you could also say it is one of the first examples in which the "balance of power" debates migrated from data to decisions. The site provides content that explains how a credit score is derived and how banks use consumer data to make lending decisions for millions of people. The FICO score helps bankers make better lending decisions; myFICO helps consumers make better personal finance decisions that improve their credit health. In some cases, consumers have used this transparency to modify their behavior and become more attractive borrowers—that is, lower-risk borrowers— which hence enables them to obtain lower interest rates.

After Fair Isaac made FICO scores available to consumers in 2001, an almost immediate result was far fewer scare stories in the media and more consumer interest in understanding the meaning of their scores. As a result of myFICO.com, Fair Isaac moved into the public eye as a company that helped people measure—and master—their credit health. Along, the way, Fair Isaac also cultivated a profitable consumer brand, offering a variety of different myFICO branded subscription services that offer consumers tools to monitor and manage their credit score.

Although articles skeptical or critical of the credit score are still common in the business media, as Fair Isaac has become more open about the FICO score, this has spawned positive and widespread personal finance media coverage. *The Wall Street Journal*, Motley Fool, *Consumer Reports*, and hundreds of publications and programs share insights for consumers to help them improve their credit score.

In 1995, the Federal National Mortgage Association (Fannie Mae) and Federal Home Loan Mortgage Corporation (Freddie Mac) endorsed the FICO score for the mortgage underwriting process. These endorsements were the trigger for mass adoption of the FICO in the mortgage industry. Four years later, in 1999, score disclosure was becoming a hot topic, particularly in California. Bills were being introduced to require lenders to disclose how scores were being calculated. That summer, Fair Isaac reached out to client companies in the business of lending and advised them that there was an unmet market need for credit score education. Even though the lenders were initially hesitant about disclosure, if Fair Isaac and the lenders did not take action, then the government was going to legislate mandatory disclosure. There was concern that this would have been negative because the government would not know how to effectively mandate meaningful consumer education.

That year, Fair Isaac approached three credit bureaus with a concept for consumer education and consumer access to the FICO score. Only Equifax expressed significant interest, so Fair Isaac and Equifax entered into a partnership. Equifax already had a consumer site, and it made FICO scores available on their website. In turn, Fair Isaac used Equifax data to provide credit reports and FICO scores on myFICO.com.

Freddie Mac worked with Fair Isaac to communicate information helpful to consumers. Fair Isaac posted all factors that go into a FICO score and worked with three credit bureaus to make this information available. In 2001, Fair Isaac launched myFICO.com to provide the first consumer access to FICO scores, and we included a significant media campaign, with stints on NBC's *The Today Show*, in connection with the launch. The myFICO.com website received three major spikes in traffic, one per hour, for three hours as *The Today Show* was broadcast across time zones.

The initial launch exceeded expectations, but future demand was hard to predict. The original concept was to break even and recover costs. Within six months, it was clear from consumer demand that there was a significant market for helping people know and understand their credit scores. Even though FICO scores can be obtained on credit bureau websites, the myFICO.com site is designed to be more consumer-friendly, thereby helping people understand how lenders make decisions.

Who Controls the "Opt-In/Opt-Out" Tool?

In theory, the idea behind opt-in and opt-out choices on the Web is that they offer a way for consumers to exercise their privacy rights. In practice, however, the model can be trickier. Companies have control of this system, because they write the rules for the default option. And the decision to make a system opt-in or opt-out, which is also a company's call, can make a significant difference to consumers if they understand the implications, which is not easy.

For example, you may recall Facebook's fumble during the 2007 holiday season with its advertising initiative called Beacon. Facebook's CEO Mark Zuckerberg, then only twenty-three years old, thought it would be a great idea to partner with big-brand companies—such as Sony, Verizon, Coca-Cola, and the National Basketball Association—to give Facebook members the chance to see their friends' every purchase and surfing move on the Web. Unfortunately, even for Facebook members, who voluntarily share more personal information than any privacy-conscious person would ever reveal directly even to their bank, Beacon's spotlight was too bright. MoveOn.org, the "democracy in action" online activists, solicited more than fifty thousand Facebook subscribers to sign a petition to enable members to opt out. Facebook did add an opt-out pop-up, but you had to be alert and quick to notice it.

The program was eventually discontinued amid consumer and negative press. Even the tech media reporters were confused. In December, after the fact, the *New York Times* and *The Wall Street Journal* ran commentary on the affair, too. One said privacy advocates wanted the opt-in option. The other said they had petitioned for opt-out. The point is, neither consumers nor tech pundits could sort out what Facebook was doing, and that doomed the program from the start.[5]

How Companies Cope with Consumer Sensitivities About Data

Privacy controls and transparency solutions, both voluntary and regulatory, are doing a good job to blunt the criticism of consumer protection groups and to curb true misuse of data. But even strategies that follow the letter of the law are still targets for consumer privacy protection advocates.

Most companies have learned that deceptive use of data (with the resulting loss of customer trust) is not worth the marginal sales it may generate. Nevertheless, trust is something companies must continually earn by being open about their data collection goals and communicating their methods. Companies often don't appreciate how little the average consumer does know about anonymity in the collection of digital transaction data. This raises red flags, even when it is not an issue. Nor do they know that companies sometimes get as much value from data that is kept anonymous as they do when a person or group is identified. It depends on the strategic objective and which types of decisions are being made. Customer segmentation models can be built from depersonalized data when the objective is to identify clusters.

For example, marketers using the online advertising strategy known as behavioral targeting analyze consumers' online activities to figure out which websites attract people with specific traits. Pepsi worked with the New York-based behavioral ad network Tacoda, Inc., to identify the best sites to place ads for Pepsi's bottled water Aquafina, by tracking the traffic on sites known to attract health-conscious consumers. Tacoda (formerly an independent firm, now part of Time Warner's AOL unit) puts together networks of thousands of diverse sites that allow for insertion of behaviorally targeted ads tailored to the interests of the specific customer clusters.

> *Most companies have learned that deceptive use of data (with the resulting loss of customer trust) is not worth the marginal sales it may generate. But trust is something companies must continually earn by being open about their data collection goals and communicating their methods.*

Even though consumers don't know it, firms like Tacoda track only the behavior of anonymous browsers, and it doesn't do analysis of an individual's private and identifiable information. Some digital ad firms that pay for names of people who use the Internet regularly to shop are working with offline data brokers to better target online advertising. *The Wall Street Journal* has reported that some digital advertising firms specializing in behavioral targeting resist this practice because they already collect plenty of anonymous information and don't want to get tangled in offline data privacy issues. Bill Grossman, the president and CEO of Revenues Sciences—one of these digital advertising firms—put it this way: "Many things in online advertising are very tempting because you know they'd be efficacious, but you know they are a bad idea because they are not consumer-friendly."[6]

Segmenting the Privacy Zealots from the Pragmatists and the Indifferent

When we are wearing our consumer hats, we certainly don't like it when we feel a company is using our personal data without our approval or permission. As with other consumer behaviors, privacy attitudes can be segmented. We break them into three categories: *zealots*, *pragmatists*, and the *indifferent*. Companies should be prepared to deal with all of these different attitudes.

Privacy zealots are people who, metaphorically speaking, want to live in a log cabin in the wilderness. They don't want anybody to know anything about them for any reason. They'll opt out of everything they can opt out of, and they pay with cash to remain anonymous. They'll never be responsive to any kind of conversation or dialogue based on what somebody thinks they know about them. At the other extreme, people who are *privacy indifferent* don't care one way or another. Most people, at least in U.S. society, are pragmatists: somewhere in between the two.

> *Privacy pragmatists need to be convinced that a company will use their data to serve them better and won't do anything sneaky.*

Corporate policies and actions should mainly address privacy pragmatists, because privacy zealots are unconvertible, and the indifferent don't care. A *privacy pragmatist* is the person who says, "I'll give my personal information to you if I'm convinced that it will do me some good and not do me any kind of harm by being used for nefarious purposes." This is where trust and transparency are most important. Privacy pragmatists need to be convinced that a company will use their data to serve them better and won't do anything sneaky.

As one former editor with a leading information technology publication said about the practices of her former employer, "I do believe companies can create value for me by using data about me. But there is a fine line between personalizing an experience and overstepping a consumer's desire for privacy and protection of personal data. Selling someone's personal information is not a good idea. It may make good financial sense, but it doesn't build trust."

There are privacy pragmatists who would be happy to pay an extra few dollars a month to eliminate pop-up ads in their favorite daily newspaper website. Privacy pragmatists know they have to give something to get something. If it is apparent that a company is using what they know about you to try to provide better, more relevant service, that feels good to the consumer. One media director summed it up this way: "If people want content that is free and are willing to look at ads and be exposed to ads in order to see content—we all understand the deal—we want to serve ads that are as relevant to people as possible."[7]

Most people are also pragmatists when it comes to data security. In these digital times, consumers accept security breaches as long as they are not personally affected. Identity theft will always be a significant problem, but the technology to control it is always improving. It is interesting to note, though, how people feel when they are involved in a corporate security breach that happens to their personal data: for example, in May 2008, Javelin Strategy & Research surveyed four hundred data breach victims, and more than half of the respondents to the online survey said the breach changed their relationship with the affected institution: "Confidence and buyer behavior are severely impacted by security breaches, with 55% of victims trusting the affected institution less, and 30% choosing to never purchase goods or services from that organization."

The best strategy for managing privacy and security is common sense. You need to balance the investments you make in people and technology with the benefits to both your customers and your company. You need to weigh all the risks to make appropriate decisions.

Conclusion

Around the world, individuals and, indeed, whole societies are thinking through how digital data is being used and should be used, and for whose benefit. In general, people understand the give and take between companies and customers that is involved in creating value from consumer data. If consumers want free content on the Web, someone has to pay for it, and for the time being, advertising is paying the bill. Consumers should have control when their personalized and identifiable data is being sold by a company they have a relationship with to marketers at another independent company.

If our vision of automated and analytical decision making is to work for companies, consumers have to be confident and comfortable that corporations are using data with integrity and caution. In this chapter, we have painted a promising picture of what some companies are doing to create new sources of customer value, using information technology, analytics, and human creativity. In this time of fast and less inhibited communication, it doesn't take advanced math to sense the tenor of customers or to learn their specific concerns and desires.

However, marketers and consumers are both feeling their way in the new digital world, and the relationship is changing. Some of the first people who signed up for MyCoke Rewards complained that the program was misleading because they found they could enter only ten codes per day. (With the ten-code-per-day limit, a person who is, say, saving their codes for several days, or entering them on behalf of their whole family may have to wait an additional day to enter any codes that exceed the daily limit.) Coca-Cola didn't change the rule, but it did post a message informing consumers of the restriction. MyCoke Rewards was also criticized by the Center for Digital Democracy, an American anti-obesity group that wants to regulate how foods are marketed to children.

We couldn't write this book, or do the work we do, if we did not accept that there is always going to be some measure of friction between for-profit businesses and the customers on whom they depend for their profits. We believe responsible and reasonable corporate use of customer data is a fair and useful tool to discover *profitable ways to serve customers better*. In the real world, relations between consumers and companies are not so harmonious; this is an opportunity for improving those relationships. As companies become more adept at using digital resources and analyzing and understanding consumer behavior, they are becoming more sensitive to the importance of *creating customer relevance* and *preserving customer trust*. For all the stories about corporate abuse of customers that journalists love to write, there are just as many stories of companies and business leaders who are genuinely interested in doing well by being fair, honest, and trustworthy with data, and being good communicators.

In Chapter Four we look at the characteristics of some of our client companies whom we call *decision leaders*. These are companies that are committed, at the enterprise level, to excellence in managing operational decisions to improve business performance in marketing and many other functions, and they are on a journey to build the technology infrastructure to support it.

4

THE DISCIPLINES OF DECISION LEADERS

The Math, Mind-Set, and Technology for Managing Decisions

As we explored in Chapter Three, the delicate balance between consumer needs and corporate profitability requires businesses to engage in a disciplined approach that maintains control over their decisions. Decision management is a discipline that addresses this balance.

It can be viewed from two perspectives. As a management discipline, it is way of thinking about the quality of decisions, deliberately and systematically. We believe thinking about decisions as business assets makes you look at decision making differently. *What are the decisions I need to make? What data do I need to make decisions? How are my decisions connected to other people's decisions? What new models are required to make better decisions?* Companies that we call *disciplined decision leaders* continually ask these questions, and they invest in decision management technologies to automate the analytics that help them improve and connect decisions at the operational level. These deliberations can filter up to top management decision making with respect to operations. For example, when companies invest in decision management technologies, senior executives who are further away from day-to-day operations can see more clearly whether a subset of business processes are working or not.

From a technology perspective, decision management encompasses a class of technology products that can take can take algorithms designed by people and run them inside computer systems.

Tom Davenport notes, "[I]n order for quantitative decisions to be implemented effectively, analysis will have to be a broad capability of employees, rather than the province of a few rocket scientists."[1]

We could not agree more. Decision management technologies make this possible.

There are decision management technologies, such as adaptive control, that continuously perform analytics inside IT systems and support the automation of decisions derived from the analytics. Sometimes the automation of analytics is just a guide for a person who is making a decision. Other times the decisions and the actions are completely automated.

In this chapter, we examine a variety of applications of decision management technology to demonstrate these points—and the rewards companies reap from deliberate, systematic, and scientific management of operational decisions. To illustrate the management discipline, along with the tools that enforce that discipline and the resulting benefits, we present the experiences of Fair Isaac clients, including Dell Financial Services (the credit division of Dell Computer, Inc.), Canadian Tire (which, despite its tire-specific name, is the largest general merchandise retailer in Canada), Capital One, and the Brazilian subsidiary of Spain's Bank Santander. Many of these companies have also developed decision management technology internally; other companies, such as Wal-Mart, are practicing decision management using technology from other vendors; but the principles of decision management they are applying through technology are the same. Over time, several themes have emerged from our clients that are most successful in creating competitive advantage and gaining profits from decision management:

- There is an executive champion, a leader who takes a systematic approach to decisions, integrates experimentation and learning into company operations, and adds a bit of creativity to the business model

- These leaders utilize sophisticated tools and frameworks to ensure that their systematic approach becomes ingrained in the company—tools such as adaptive control to facilitate experimentation, decision models and efficient frontier principles to be creative in overcoming conflicting objectives, and *decision yields* to center the organization on the business benefits of better decisions. (A decision yield is the sum benefit of an organization's improved and automated decision making that results in increased revenue, reduced costs, and reduced risks.)

- The leaders approach advances in decision management as a journey: one that contains building blocks leading to greater levels of sophistication and success over time; one that is based on discovery as they make that journey, rather than a search for a finite destination.

Building a Decision Management Infrastructure

Large companies have invested billions of dollars in data warehouses and enterprise applications—such as enterprise resource planning (ERP) and customer relationship management (CRM)—to capture internal business process–level data. They have also either automated in-house or outsourced those administrative processes, such as employee benefits management, that are necessary to run the business but do not contribute to competitive advantage or business innovation. But they have not invested in the decision management technology to imbed and automate analytic models in more business processes, such as marketing and customer service, that directly affect the customer and are a source of competitive advantage. One reason is that companies have focused more on improving processes than they have on improving decisions. Another reason is that until recently the technology to automate decision management tools was not that advanced. Fair Isaac was a pioneer before it was a leader in predictive analytics, but it did not begin to create automated systems to run its analytic products until the 1970s.

Investing in Decision Management Technology Is a Journey

Figure 4.1 shows how Fair Isaac describes the decision management journey and its progression. When we present the concept for our technology architecture for decision management, we give them the complete picture of an infrastructure that automates, improves, and connects decisions. However, building the complete architecture can take several years, and many of our clients start with applications in a single function or business process before expanding further. There are three key steps on the journey, each requiring different levels of technology, analytic sophistication, and organizational commitment and connectivity. Let's take a closer look at each one.

Figure 4.1 The Decision Management Journey

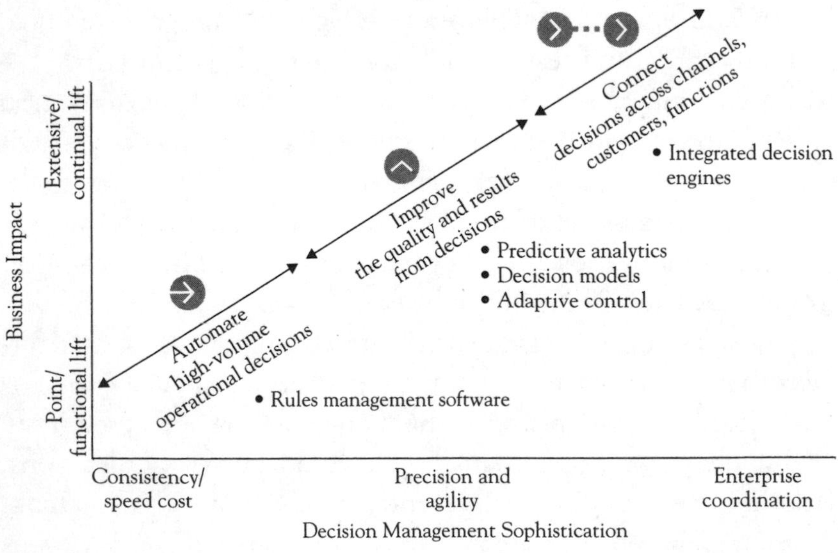

Source: Fair Isaac

Stage 1: Developing Rules-Based Systems

Companies commonly start the journey with rules-based systems, because they don't necessarily need analytics. This first stage is to automate high-volume operational decisions to make the decisions consistent and to increase control. With a basic rules management capability, a company can execute policies and procedures and can easily change the rules, too. They no longer have to update policy manuals or retrain hundreds or thousands of workers.

Stage 2: Using Predictive Analytics Models

A second stage in the journey is getting to new levels of improvement, which typically begins with the incorporation of predictive analytic models into your operating environment. As we will show in this chapter, decision models and efficient frontier frameworks mathematically evaluate trade-offs among conflicting objectives, then execute decisions. Adaptive control is both the source of key performance data and the execution engine for decision models. It captures which decisions were made for which customers, which actions were taken, the corresponding consumer behavior and reactions, and the impact on profitability. Banks have extensive experience using adaptive control to manage *individual* accounts, but only a small number of advanced leaders has used it to manage the *total value* of the customer and risk exposure.

Using decision management technology to inform, guide, or drive the decisions of frontline workers in a call center or the collections operation in a bank is a powerful way to make them more efficient and effective. Using information, key predictions, and suggested actions, these employees can make a high volume of decisions, faster and better.

> *Banks have extensive experience using adaptive control to manage individual accounts, but only a small number of advanced leaders has used it to manage the total value of the customer and risk exposure.*

Stage 3: Connecting Decisions Across Multiple Dimensions

A more advanced stage in the journey is connecting decisions across multiple dimensions of a business, including products lines, functions, channels, and geographies. Receiving a call from a bank's debt collection department is not exactly the kind of experience customers want to have, but if the process is handled well, they will appreciate it. Consider the following example.

Raiffeisen Bank is a member of Raiffeisen International, one of the largest banking groups in Central and Eastern Europe. In 2003 it established a standardized decision system for collections that connects decision making across fifteen Central and Eastern European countries (in multiple languages and currencies) and across a full selection of consumer loan products. It also allows for local optimization in a controlled manner. Each country employs about thirty-five distinct collection decision strategies, such as prioritizing accounts based on different risk levels or different steps in the decision flow. By automating many of the decisions, it is able to handle this volume with *half* the number of collectors it would have needed without the system.

For Millennium BCP, Portugal's largest bank, the journey involved deploying a consistent set of capabilities to support a "connected" multicountry expansion across Europe and Africa. As it expanded, the bank standardized and automated processes to enhance efficiency in managing its retail portfolios abroad. Over time, the bank moved from stand-alone predictive models to more sophisticated decision models, and it applied adaptive control to more and more decision areas.

What Are the Disciplines of Decision Leaders?

In our view, companies that are making the leap from *drowning in data* to learning from transactions and interactions to improve their business's processes and their business's results share the following characteristics:

- They are systematic and quantitative.
- They are always learning and improving.
- They are bold and creative.

Automation also changes the type of decisions you are making from day to day or how you make decisions, depending on what your job is. Working with analytics and other decision management technologies encourages you to experiment more and discover more about how you can create business value. Automation of models that are always learning and improving, such as adaptive control, institutionalizes these qualities in an organization. Obviously, using data on consumer behavior as a starting point to make predictions that drive decisions is very systematic and quantitative. Let's take a closer look at each one of these characteristics.

Discipline #1: Decision Leaders Are Systematic and Quantitative

Analytics gives decision makers in operational business roles more precise ways to compare multiple business objectives (for example, *profit per customer* versus *growth in market share*). Decision models identify the ideal action to take for a particular transaction or interaction with a customer. Being systematic and quantitative is more than doing the math and using automation to make better decisions faster. It is also about excellence in managing a company's decision yield. The decision yield is measured along five dimensions:

1. *Precision:* the company makes more profitable and targeted decisions.
2. *Consistency:* the company makes decisions in the same way across channels, business units, and geographies.

3. *Agility:* the company makes decisions while being able to adapt on the fly.

4. *Cost:* the company makes decisions in a more automated manner and with less work steps to reduce operating costs.

5. *Speed:* the company makes decisions at real-time speeds that accelerate business processes.

> *Tesco carefully monitors its redemption rates for direct marketing initiatives and then makes small process changes to improve response rates—which have enabled Tesco to achieve a 20-percent response rate, in stark contrast to the grocery industry average of a measly 2 to 3 percent.*

We discuss the decision yield in more detail later in this chapter.

As shown in Chapter Two, companies like Capital One, Tesco, and Harrah's excel at understanding how to manage high volumes of operational decisions with mathematical precision to increase and sustain profitability. In direct marketing, Tesco outclasses all of its competitors in the grocery business. For example, Tesco uses its data to carefully monitor its redemption rates for direct-marketing initiatives, and then makes small adjustments to its strategy, gleaned through analytics, that increase response rates dramatically. In direct marketing Tesco is able to achieve a 20-percent response rate, in stark contrast to the grocery industry average of a measly 2 to 3 percent.

The output of the models that statistical analysts use is made accessible to many people throughout companies through computer automation. This accessibility to analytics is especially valuable to support middle managers and frontline workers.

For example, Wal-Mart is known for its precision supply chain management, yet the company is also a leader in making information generated by math and computer wizards accessible and useful to people throughout its organization. Computers displaying screen visualizations and representations of data processed through complex equations guide the decision making of thousands of Wal-Mart employees who are responsible for every-day decisions that affect profitability and customers.

While Wal-Mart may be making decisions regarding which products to place in which store locations, other decisions may be much more granular, dependent on individual consumer behavior, and integrated into operations. As mentioned in Chapter One, Capital One had enough information on its customers to fill the hard drives of more than two hundred thousand personal comput-ers. More important, this is how the bank *uses* that information:

> People call to ask about their MasterCard balance, or whether a recent payment was received, or why their interest rate has jumped. And more than 1 million times a week, here's what happens—before a caller hears the first ring: The instant the last digit is punched, high-speed computers swing into action. Loaded with background information on one in seven U.S. households and with exhaustive data about how the company's millions of customers behave, the computers identify who is calling and predict the reason for the call.

> After reviewing 50 options for whom to notify, the computers pick the best option for each situation. The computers also pull and pass along about two-dozen pieces of information about the person who is calling. They even predict what the caller might want to buy—even though he or she isn't calling to buy anything—and then they prepare the customer-service rep to sell that item, once the original reason for the call has been addressed. All of these steps—the incoming call, the data review, the analysis, the rout-ing, and the recommending—happen in just 100 milliseconds.[2]

It is the frontline workers who make the most indelible cus-tomer impressions. And when they're armed with analytics, frontline staff can get instant information to answer questions they face all the time, including these:

- Should I accept this customer's return?
- Should I order more components now or next month?

- Should I suggest this customer consider some other products he or she hasn't asked about?

With an increase in customer self-service and web-based sales, these types of decisions are being fully data-driven. The result is that people serving and interacting with customers every day are making better decisions, and they are likely happier because analytics makes their job more interesting and empowers them.

When Capital One first developed its systems to integrate analytics into its information technology architecture, it was a pioneer in managing business processes, information technology, and analytics to elevate the quality of decision making throughout an enterprise. Automating analytic models to deliver insights, predictions, and decisions to guide frontline workers is just one of the elements of disciplined decision management.

Discipline #2: Decision Leaders Are Always Learning and Improving

Most of the companies we have worked with or observed are systematic and quantitative in seeking one-time business improvements. Unfortunately, far fewer companies commit themselves to the discipline of *continual* learning and improvement of key consumer decisions over a multiyear horizon. But continual learning is critical, which is another reason Tesco has been so successful, as consultant Clive Humby noted: "One of the accepted principles of [Tesco's] program is that there is no such thing as complete success or total failure. Everything that happens to Clubcard is seen as an opportunity to learn, to refine, to improve, and move on."[3]

Discipline #3: Decision Leaders Are Bold and Creative

Before Capital One did mass customization of credit cards, it had never been done. Now, of course, it's a standard way to compete.

Similarly, as shown in Chapter Two, Best Buy's use of customer segmentations to change its store formats was considered a revolutionary idea when it was proposed. In fact, until the customer segmentation work helped Best Buy's executives visualize the customer experience differ-

> *Best Buy's use of customer segmentations to change its store formats was considered a revolutionary idea when it was proposed . . . . Being bold and creative is critical.*

ently, they had not even considered suggesting a change in store format to provide a personalized experience across all channels. Being bold and creative is critical.

Case Study: How Canada's Largest Retail Chain Identified Its Highest-Risk Credit Customers—and Reduced Its Losses

Some of our clients have demonstrated the ability to examine their key business problems from a fresh perspective that leads to trying a novel approach to improvement. In this case example, the leadership clearly demonstrated the key disciplines of being systematic, always learning, and applying creativity. In the 1990s, when J. P. Martin was with Canadian Tire (a client of ours that has been on our advisory board; he is now a senior risk management executive in the card services division of J.P. Morgan Chase Bank of Canada), he hypothesized that existing customer credit risk predictions based on past payment behavior could be substantially improved by incorporating detailed purchasing behavior as well. His deeper conjecture was that purchasing behavior might reveal patterns of nuanced, responsible behavior that were not already captured by consumers' past payment behavior.

Canadian Tire is Canada's largest retail chain: it comprises 265 gas stations that also offer carwash services, as well as 475 general merchandise stores that sell automotive parts and services, home products, sports and leisure products, and unisex casual clothing. The financial services unit of Canadian Tire

developed predictive models for credit risk based on retail transaction data from its own stores and external merchant category
information. By analyzing purchases of eighty-five thousand
diverse stock keeping units (SKUs) in its database, the model
differentiated between high- and low-risk credit card customers
strictly on the basis of their purchases. For example:

- People who bought transmission sealer were viewed as
  higher credit risk, perhaps because the person had chosen
  to buy the sealer rather than spend hundreds of dollars
  more to fix the problem.
- People who purchased carbon monoxide monitors and
  smoke alarms were assessed by the model as conscientious
  homeowners, and were therefore viewed as *lower credit risk*.
- People who bought products like a titanium drill set or a
  woodworking set, which indicated expensive hobbies, were
  also seen as *lower credit risks*.

The financial services unit also analyzed 60 million transactions at over 210 different merchants across Canada. Like the
SKU model, merchant modeling proved highly predictive. For
example, the credit risk profile of jewelry store patrons was significantly lower than that of regulars at pool halls.

Over time, Canadian Tire has used this fine-tuned understanding of their customer base to make better operational decisions,
such as which marketing promotions to make to which customers and which credit terms to offer to which customers. This has
enabled Canadian Tire to maintain strong customer relationships
and continue its path of 10-percent-plus earnings growth despite
strong competition as Wal-Mart and others expand into Canada.

Seeking (Not Maximizing) Profit Under the Weight of Real-World Constraints

Managers are often seduced into believing that optimal business performance is achieved by maximizing profits. But it is
not that simple. Improved business performance is *fully* realized
only when managers recognize and address the importance of

key business metrics—as well as possible conflicts among those key business metrics. Put another way, companies are not *profit maximizers*; rather, they are constrained *profit seekers*. There are a number of tools and techniques to further this cause; we have chosen three that have a high degree of impact:

> By analyzing purchases of eighty-five thousand diverse products in its database, the model differentiated between high- and low-risk credit card customers strictly on the basis of their purchases. . . . For example, the credit risk profile of jewelry store patrons was significantly lower than that of regulars at pool halls.

- Adaptive control—a software tool that facilitates experimentation and learning by enabling business leaders to test new decisions in a real-world operating environment
- Decision models and efficient frontier—an analytic technique to evaluate conflicting trade-offs driven by those pesky constraints
- Decision yield—a business framework for categorizing and evaluating business benefits

Using the Adaptive Control Technique: Experimenting with Alternative Decisions to Make the Best Possible Decision

As mentioned in Chapter One, in the 1980s Fair Isaac introduced adaptive control, an automated analytic technology, to the credit card industry. Adaptive control (also known in the world of systems theory as *dual control*) refers to the twofold objective of simultaneously:

1. Making the *best possible decisions* to control a complex system based on current knowledge
2. Experimenting with *alternative decisions* to learn more about a system's behavior, in order to control it more effectively in the future

The software is *adaptive* in that business leaders can test changes to their decisions and compare results to the existing operational baseline, and it is a *control* mechanism in that the tests are run on a subset of the customer base until it is proven to be a better decision strategy, at which time it can be rolled out to 100 percent of the customer population in a controlled manner.

Although credit scores measure the risk of increasing a given line of credit to a customer, adaptive control tests the effects of different strategies on different business objectives *before a manager fully commits to a course of action for his or her decisions*. Adaptive control technology automates the translation of those decision strategies into specific, individual customer actions, automates the use of complex predictive analysis in taking those actions, and automates the random selection of a subset of trial customer accounts from real customer accounts.

For example, a typical decision might be how much to increase the credit line on a particular group of accounts or which set of customers should be targeted for a new credit card offer. The technology learns by trying out different strategies. Then, with mathematical precision, it identifies the *best strategies* for different segments of customers based on factors such as their credit score, their spending patterns, and other criteria.

Fair Isaac first tried adaptive control on Montgomery Ward's credit operation. Executives responsible for this process were interested in doing a better job of setting and adjusting credit limits for its store card customers. After assigning an initial credit limit based on the information on the credit application, they would adjust those limits only when a customer requested a credit limit increase. That required a new application that completely ignored the purchase and payment record of the customer. The idea was to develop an algorithm to predict future credit risk based on past purchase and payment behavior (a behavior score) to decide by how much to increase customer credit limits—and to do so proactively instead of waiting for customers to request an increase.

Although it was clear that high-scoring accounts (signifying low credit risk) could more safely be given increases, no one knew by how much. The application of adaptive control tested the effects of different credit line increases on randomly selected accounts, as a function of behavior scores. Over 90 percent of customers remained in the control group and were treated in the usual mode. After the experiment was conducted, various business measures were observed over time: purchase activities, balance build-ups, delinquency levels. The results of the experiments were startlingly better than the old business-as-usual strategy.

"The Champion versus the Challenger": Determining Which Strategy Is Best

The adaptive control software can be applied to any number of decision strategies, whether it be which offers to promote to customers, how much credit to extend, or which contact method to use. These decisions have a number of variables that can be tested, and a horse race is a good metaphor to illustrate the essential ideas of adaptive control. In a horse race, a champion is challenged by several different horses in a race measured based on one metric—the fastest time to the finish line. But if you are going to judge whether Strategy A for how to increase your customers' credit line is better than Strategy B, you need to report the differences in performance of *all* metrics that are important to your business—for example, your profit, your losses, and your total transaction volume. Fair Isaac uses the term *champion/challenger* to describe how an adaptive control system assesses every dimension of business performance to determine which horse (that is, which strategy) wins the race:

- The *champion* strategy is the best set of actions to take for different customer segments, based on what the particular company knows about its accounts at any given moment.

- *Challenger* strategies test the best new ideas on how to do better than the current champion strategy.

For an example, let's return to the case of Montgomery Ward: the vast majority of accounts in a typical test were treated as the Champion, and a relatively small fraction of accounts were routed to one or more Challenger strategies. In a continual, disciplined search for business improvement, new Challenger strategies are often informed by analysis from a previous race. Thus, a new cycle of adaptive testing and controlled learning is initiated.

Case Study: How a Multinational Bank Used Several Challenger Strategies to Increase Revenue and Reduce Its Exposure to Risky Customers

The Brazilian subsidiary of the Santander banking group used the champion/challenger method to operate in a high-growth consumer credit market. The Santander Group is a 150-year-old bank and one of the world's leading banks (by market capitalization), with a market value of €9.5 billion (as of the end of 2007); it is also the number one bank in the euro zone. It has more than 11,000 locations, 65 million customers, 2.3 million shareholders, and 132,000 employees.

From 1998 to 2006, credit card transaction volumes for the Brazilian banking market rose by 230 percent: in 2006, there were two billion transactions, worth US$75 billion. In 2005, Santander sought us out, wanting to take advantage of our adaptive control technology to manage this revenue growth in a more profitable manner, which was an ideal fit given the high growth rates and relatively volatile economic conditions. One of the decisions that it focused on was whether or not to approve a credit card transaction if the customer was over his or her credit limit.

Santander's *champion* strategy was to approve everything up to a standard over-limit percentage (for example, up to 10 percent over the limit for any one account). In addition, a new *challenger* strategy was introduced that varied the limits based on product type, risk score, days delinquent, and other factors. This "challenger 1" decision strategy was applied to 20 percent of the Brazilian bank's customer population, and it yielded 25 percent more revenue per transaction, while reducing delinquencies by 47 percent.

By giving a higher credit limit to customers with better credit risk profiles, the bank increased revenues while lowering its exposure to less credit-worthy customers. In short, it achieved its goal of higher transaction volumes and lowered its risk exposure. This successful strategy was then applied to the bank's entire customer population.

After a few months, the business decided to run a new test: a "challenger 2" strategy. This fine-tuned the over-limit decisions even further by adding another decision criteria: length of time as a customer.

The result? Fantastic! By the end of 2006, Santander Brazil's credit card operation had completed a total of four tests, and it achieved an 8 percent additional increase in transaction dollars, while reducing delinquencies by 50 percent, as shown in Figure 4.2.

Charting the Efficient Frontier to Navigate Among Conflicting Objectives

Adaptive control is useful for creating and managing decision strategies with a focused goal. On rare occasions, competing decision strategies can be evaluated on the basis of a single business metric—for example, profit contribution. In this case, the best decision strategy can be determined by the one metric that maximizes profit contribution. However, in the vast majority of situations, decision makers care about *multiple*

> In the vast majority of situations, decision makers care about multiple *business objectives*—which usually are also conflicting *objectives*.

Figure 4.2 Santander's Champion/Challenger Test of Its Risk Exposure to Delinquent Credit Card Customers

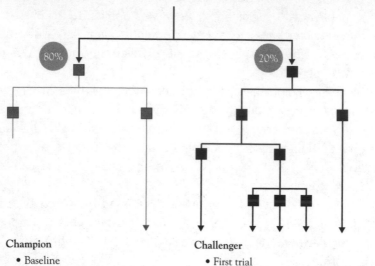

Champion
- Baseline
- Standard over-limit percentage for all accounts in good standing

Challenger
- First trial
- Vary the over-limit percentage by product type, customer risk level, and so on.

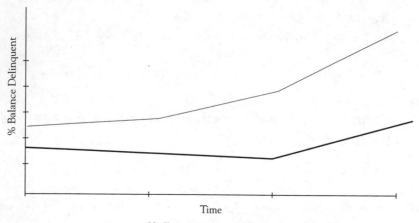

Challenger's improved performance
- 50% decrease in delinquencies
- 8% increase in transaction dollars

Source: Fair Isaac

business objectives—which usually are also *conflicting* objectives. For example, under some conditions, increasing the company's market share might be a higher priority than increasing its profit, but under other conditions, the opposite might be true. It is these conflicting objectives that require something in addition to adaptive control to effectively navigate them toward the most profit.

What's crucial is to select a decision strategy that strikes wise *trade-offs* under different conditions, among multiple objectives. An *efficient frontier* represents the most favorable possible trade-offs. Your responsibility (if you're the decision maker) is to select an operating point on the efficient frontier that best serves your business under current business conditions.

For example, Figure 4.3 uses a credit line increase strategy to show how decision modeling reveals the location and the shape of the efficient frontier. Without this analysis, a business will operate inefficiently (inside the frontier) relative to its potential. Most businesses have identified conflicting objectives but fail to

Figure 4.3 An Efficient Frontier Based on a Credit Line Model

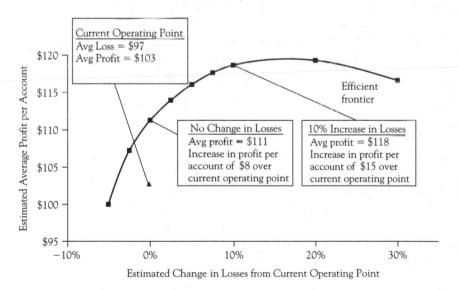

Source: Fair Isaac

mathematically represent them. Without using techniques such as decision modeling and efficient frontiers, these businesses are essentially flying blind.

> The efficient frontier and adaptive control tools give decision makers in operational business roles more precise ways to compare multiple—and often competing—business objectives (for example, profit per customer versus growth in market share).

Using Decision Yield to Consider All Dimensions of Business Benefit

What constitutes a good decision? Is it the outcome? The cost of executing a decision? The speed of executing a decision? How well are decisions coordinated among different parts of an organization? When we work with clients to measure the effectiveness of their automated decision making, we use the *decision yield* tool. As discussed earlier, the five dimensions of decision yield (shown in Figure 4.4) are a comprehensive way to evaluate how decision management can contribute to better business performance. Let's look at each of these dimensions in a bit more detail.

Figure 4.4 Decision Yield: The Key Dimensions for Decision Improvement

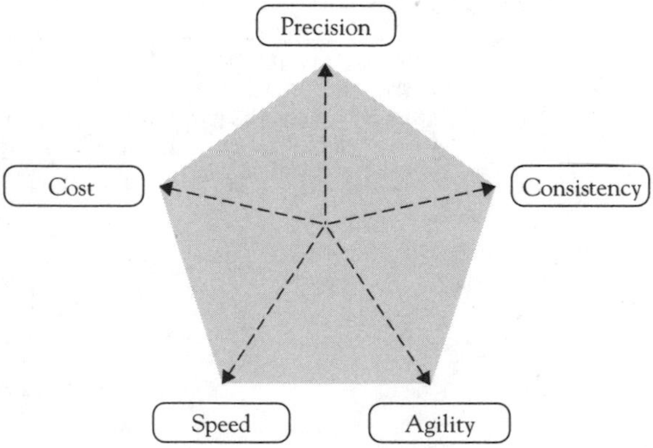

Source: Fair Isaac

1. *Precision*. Sophisticated analytic technology is all about the degree of accuracy with which you can predict the outcome of a decision. The difference between a $1,000 or $2,000 increase on credit lines of ten thousand customers could be a shot in the dark, or you could use an analytic model to compare revenue and losses for both options.

2. *Consistency*. Inside large companies, consistency reduces costs and complexity. Many different types of decisions may need to be consistent across channels, business units, and geographies. Consistency in brand messages and actions improves customer satisfaction. Consistency in decision making across lines of business can prevent cannibalization of one unit by another.

3. *Agility*. Agility is a measure of a company's ability to change decisions fast. These days, most companies put a premium on being able to adapt quickly to all kinds of changes in the business environment.

4. *Cost*. This is about reducing the expense associated with developing, executing, and managing decisions—especially, reducing the number of human interventions required through automating manual decisions or removing processing steps but making the correct decision in-stream with a customer interaction.

5. *Speed*. Whatever the point of contact is with a company—that is, whether it's in a bricks-and-mortar store, on the Internet, or at a self-service kiosk—customers notice when they are served fast and well. In almost all consumer businesses, speed and accuracy are the most important factors affecting customer satisfaction. In 2006, Booz & Co. surveyed more than 1,200 customers of companies in four industries—retail banking, brokerage, health insurance, and airlines—and asked them to rate the importance of eight customer service elements. Speed was number one.[4]

We have applied the concept of decision yield extensively in the insurance industry and have noticed that our clients tend to focus on one primary benefit while at the same time striving to realize secondary benefits across all areas. For example, one of the major drivers in insurance underwriting is precision, or improving the targeted risk profile and the granularity of tiers used in accepting customers, which has led to a 20-percent profit improvement over several years for one insurer and an 18-percent profit improvement in the first year of use for another.

Combining rules management software with predictive analytics in insurance has also led to gains in speed, consistency, agility, and cost. From a speed perspective, one insurer shifted its policy applications to a real-time online experience and was able to increase by six times the number of customers completing online application requests. Another insurer that we will highlight in a later chapter cut costs of manually reviewing policy applications by 99 percent as it went from 100 percent of all policies being manually reviewed to only 1 percent being manually reviewed, with the remaining 99 percent processed automatically. Many insurers have incorporated consistency into their decision improvements, with a focus on consistent use of regulatory rules that vary across all fifty U.S. states in the underwriting process, while at the same time lowering IT costs. And a number have gained strategic benefit from increased agility; for example, one insurer standardized the decision processes, which enabled it to expand business with direct and independent agents by 35 percent while maintaining the same staff levels.

Case Study: How Dell Financial Services Coordinated Its Risk and Marketing Decisions

Greater computing power and data access is raising the yield on automated decision making. More decisions can be in real time or near-real time, but companies still have difficulty coordinating decision strategies between departments and changing decisions as the strategy changes. This was the challenge for Dell Financial Services (DFS), the in-house consumer credit arm of the computer manufacturer Dell, Inc.

DFS set a business objective to grow PC sales by offering favorable financing deals to attract new customers. The marketing and risk groups each had their own decision criteria for accepting or rejecting an applicant, but often these criteria were in conflict. For example, a college-age male who buys a high-end PC and upgrades his software frequently looks like a *great prospect* to marketing: he's young and into games, and he has high potential lifetime revenue value if Dell can hold onto his business. However, for the risk group, this same customer looked *less attractive,* because he had no credit history and limited income. Aggressive fraud screens made many of these young customers ineligible for the special financing.

Because the marketing and risk departments were not coordinating their decisions, the criteria for targeting offers to new customers were changed randomly, depending on which function had more sway—for example:

- When losses from fraud were rising, the *risk group* would *ratchet up* its controls, which reduced revenues.
- When pressure mounted to grow revenues, *marketing* would demand that the fraud controls *be more lenient* to qualify more customers.

Finally, DFS changed the decision approach to measure the *lifetime value of the customer,* and the company created decision criteria so that people with relatively low risk for fraud were not eliminated. Ultimately, DFS built an automated decision management system to analyze each credit application, taking into consideration all of the following factors:

- Fraud
- Financial risk
- Lifetime value
- Product configuration
- Marketing and promotion decisions

For example, different mathematical models in the system do fraud checks, credit risk analysis, and customer segmentations. The new system also monitors decisions, using adaptive control systems to continually improve strategies over time.

If you think about the Dell financial services story in the context of an efficient frontier, you'll note that before it changed its decision management system none of Dell's baseline decisions were near the efficient frontier. Decisions would swing like a pendulum between random decisions, depending on which functional leader, such as marketing or risk, had the most power. This led to either *sagging revenue* or *soaring losses* later. As it is all too common in business, DFS managers did not have the tools to understand the trade-offs between risk and revenue, so they did not know how their decisions were affecting the other objective.

Conclusion

Although there are few companies operating today that could not benefit from some investments in analytic technology, there are certain types of companies that can benefit more than others. Like any technology investment, you start with the basic questions:

- In what ways do you want your company to be superior?
- Under what circumstances could your company live with parity or at a disadvantage compared to your competitors?

This is how senior leaders invest resources wisely. If your company is good on service, typically it is not competing on lowest price. But as we have demonstrated in previous chapters, analytic tools can enable you to improve your company's service propositions without adding operating costs that can adversely affect your company's prices.

Naturally, there will be circumstances in which, for the particular industry or the nature of the business, analytics and decision management are less likely to be sources of competitive advantage; to illustrate here are two contrasting examples:

- *Consumer and small business lenders* lead other subsectors of the financial services industries in their use of analytics.
- In contrast, in *middle-market corporate lending,* analytics is less useful, because commercial lenders are not drowning in data and their client base is more homogenous and small relative to the millions of consumers retail banks serve.

Furthermore, the decisions of executive leaders can make a big difference. For example, back in the 1990s, when Capital One was transforming its business by investing in decision management technology and analytic talent, MBNA—one of Capital One's major competitors—did not. Instead, MBNA went with its superiority in *affinity marketing* because its leadership believed MBNA was attracting high-quality credit customers without analytics. MBNA did not aspire to compete with Cap One, analytic for analytic. However, MBNA also did not ignore the capability completely. If Cap One aspired to get an "A" in analytics, MBNA felt it could do just fine with a gentleman's "C." There are a number of factors that determine performance over time, but we believe that Cap One's "A" has allowed them to deliver performance levels sufficient to remain independent, whereas MBNA was eventually acquired.

Overall, however, we believe there are a certain class of companies and certain industries for which decision management is becoming "the ante that gives companies the right to play the game" (as Ian Davis put it, quoted in the Introduction to this book). These are companies that have millions of customers with whom they interact constantly—that is, business-to-consumer companies. For these companies, the precision of decision management can be significant—a modest improvement in the quality of a key decision strategy can translate into large improvements in profits or can prevent big losses. This is the case with credit cards, and with consumer financial services in general. Decision management can also make a huge difference in performance for companies in industries that operate with razor-thin margins, such as grocery retailing.

Decision management gives a company the tools to continually gain and retain new customer knowledge, so it can be more precise and relevant in what it markets and sells to them.

If a company is growing fast, analytics can accelerate and even supercharge its growth. Consumer companies going after higher sales and market share are acquiring new customers rapidly. Analytics are important to making their customer care services more effective. When customers are new, companies don't know much about them, but if keeping customers is the goal, decision management gives a company the tools to continually gain and retain new customer knowledge, so it can be more precise and relevant in what it markets and sells to them.

At the executive level, to be a decision leader as an organization, you need individuals who promote the three disciplines, and you need a mix of people who have the skills and the personalities to create value from the technology. With this in mind, in Chapter Five we discuss how to optimize the value of analytical people for business success.

5

THE NEW KNOWLEDGE WORKERS

Defining the Talent Mix for Success with Analytics

Having the right leadership disciplines and reinforcing those disciplines through technology is half the battle. Yet there is one remaining significant organizational challenge: having sufficient talent throughout the organization that can capitalize on opportunities to further automate, improve, and connect decisions. This chapter describes the different jobs of analytic professionals; shows where analytic people work—that is, in which departments or across departments—in different companies; and offers case studies from companies as varied as Harrah's and India's largest bank. These insights should help executives plan their own career paths, develop the right mix of skills in their teams, and organize decision management talent to deliver the best results possible.

Analytic Professionals Are the New Knowledge Workers

Peter Drucker was the greatest predictor of management trends in the twentieth century: back in 1959, he originated the term *knowledge worker*, which is ubiquitous in business today. In 2001, at the age of ninety-one, Drucker forecast a new worker for the twenty-first century, which he called the *knowledge technologist*.[1] His definition is not what you might expect: "These people are as much manual workers as they are knowledge workers . . . In fact, they usually spend far more time working with their hands than with their brains. But their manual work is based on a substantial amount of theoretical knowledge that can be acquired only through formal education, not through an apprenticeship. They are not, as a rule, much better paid than traditional skilled workers, but they see themselves as 'professionals.'"[2]

Analytics, information technology, decision management, and business skills will blend together, especially as the generations who grew up with computers progress in their careers.

Taking some liberty with Drucker's definition of a knowledge technologist, we use the term *decision native* to describe a variety of new professionals who, in the context of decision management, are filling unprecedented demand by corporations for information technology–savvy, left-brain/right-brain thinkers. According to Christopher Vollmer, the leader of Booz & Co.'s North American media and entertainment practice, "The exploding availability of digitally driven consumer data has transformed marketing into a new frontier application for business mathematics. Just as mathematics revolutionized finance, it is reinvigorating marketing, as new models and algorithms extract value from consumer and business databases."[3]

Analytics will likely follow a path similar to that of IT, starting as a stand-alone functional unit in the organization. But eventually, analytics, information technology, decision management, and business skills will blend together, especially as the generations who grew up with computers progress in their careers. There are now at least three generations of digital natives in the business world:

- The youngest baby boomers—who were the first to use PCs in the office
- The Gen X managers—who take computers as much for granted as their elders did telephones and fax machines

- The Gen Y managers—who have never worked without the Internet

These three generations of managers and executives will change how business decisions in companies of all sizes are made and managed. People with a wide variety of backgrounds are filling a wide variety of jobs that require advanced mathematics and computer skills.

Information Architects: Where Strategy, Data, and Technology Meet

Ning (which means peace in Chinese), Slide (which is self-explanatory), and Meebo (which means whatever you want) are three hot California-based Web 2.0 companies founded since 2004. Meebo Inc. launched in 2005, with a novel new instant messaging service, to give users the ability to have live conversations through the Web without the need for desktop software.

Seth Sternberg, one of three founders of Meebo and also its CEO, created the role of *information architect* because weekly strategy meetings always ended with someone asking for more data before a decision was made. Sternberg describes an information architect as "someone who is good at data analytics and has network administrator experience."[4] Equally important is that information architects need to be able "to extrapolate data trends into written reports that everyone can understand."[5] Bob Lee, a thirty-something former engineer at Apple, was Meebo's first info architect hire. "I think of the raw data as stone, and I am sculpting it, trying to pull something of use from it."[6]

Data is an important raw material required to grow decision capabilities, which is why this role is so important. Information architects place an emphasis on this raw material as an asset—acquiring, growing, and integrating data to drive better decisions.

Number-Crunching Creatives Blend Analytics with the Art of Marketing

Booz & Co.'s Chris Vollmer calls the new digital data-driven breed of advertising and marketing executives "number-crunching creatives." They emerged in dot-coms, ad agencies, and large old-line brand companies, and demand for their imaginations and their math skills is growing rapidly throughout the corporate world, in all types of companies and industries. Basem Nayfeh is one example: he's the chief technology officer of Revenue Science, a small behavioral targeting firm, and a Stanford classmate of Google cofounder Sergey Brin. Nayfeh is surprised to be working where he is: "If you had asked any of us 5 or even 10 years ago if we would be in advertising, none of us would have said yes."[7]

Marketers' greatest need is to deepen their understanding of consumer behavior and use analytics to calculate return on investment.

In 2006, Booz & Co. and the Association of National Advertisers conducted a survey of 250 senior marketers to find out how interactive marketing had changed their priorities. Two-thirds of the respondents said marketers' greatest need is to deepen their understanding of consumer behavior and use analytics to calculate return on investment (ROI). Similarly, in 2005, Forrester Research forecast an increase in ROI analytics among consumer packaged-goods companies, retail, auto, finance, and pharmaceutical companies.[8] All this implies a very new career trajectory for marketers: one that is customer data–driven, proactive, and strategic.

Corporate demand is rising for people who are "bilingual": that is, they "speak business" yet are simultaneously facile users of statistical techniques and software technology.

Marketing executives at these large consumer companies can use analytics to proactively simulate and optimize spending allocations at the macro level using micro-level data. Rather than doing the analysis of ROI on spending after the decisions are made, marketers use models as a planning tool to make big budgetary decisions—such as whether to fund a broad web-based interactive marketing campaign or to personalize a campaign, using text messaging to mobile phones. The data used will move from aggregate sales to individual consumer behavior.

The MBAs and the Mathematicians: Where Strategists and Scientists Meet

Sometimes, what's needed is a combo of technologist, statistician, and MBA, or some variation. Never before have companies needed these varied sets of experience to be combined in one person. For example, people who have degrees in operations research have the computing and analytic knowledge and they have Ph.D.s, but they don't have MBAs. However, although the combination of an MBA and a mathematics background is rare, corporate demand is rising for people who are "bilingual": that is, they "speak business" yet are simultaneously facile users of statistical techniques and software technology. Furthermore, the most valuable people are those who are "trilingual": that is, their languages are computing, analytics, and business.

Basic training in business school has always been about sharpening the analytical minds of future managers. But before complicated algorithms and sophisticated simulations, business math was much simpler. For more than three hundred years, besides the abacus, the slide rule proved satisfactory to do the necessary calculation to make analytical business decisions. The first class of fifty-nine students entering the Harvard Business School in 1908 used slide rules. So did the classes of 1946, 1956, and 1966. Baby boomers who attended business schools in the United States and Europe in the late 1960s and 1970s began using pocket calculators to run their numbers on net present value, bond amortizations, and depreciation rates. A few computer geeks may have spent late nights in a computer lab, but the keyboards most familiar to an American MBA in the

1970s and, even into the 1980s, were on a typewriter and a Texas Instruments calculator.

Computing added a new level of ease in performing calculations but also more complexity. In the digital age, students attending undergraduate and graduate business schools around the world—in New York and New Delhi, in Cambridge and Caracas, in Palo Alto and São Paulo—still carry calculators in their pockets. But there are many more aspiring business professionals who have the math and computer skills to match the era we live in. These are people who are as comfortable talking about Bayesian influence diagrams and genetic algorithms as they are with calculating the bottom line.

There is also a new generation of business professionals who are getting master's degrees in what is referred to as *financial mathematics*. For example, Stanford University's master's program in financial mathematics is an interdisciplinary collaboration among business school faculty and the departments of mathematics, economics and management, and science and engineering. Stanford undergraduates can choose an interdisciplinary major called "Values, Technology, Science and Society," a collection of courses concerned with how society plans for advances in science and technology. The premise of the program is that technological progress usually runs well ahead of society's ability to benefit. Not an entirely new concept—after all (as described in Chapter One), this was true of the weaponry and military technology that Bill Fair and Earl Isaac analyzed as operations researchers at Stanford Research Institute in the 1950s. It is also true of today's evolving information technologies.

The decision sciences are a variety of new interdisciplinary graduate academic programs; they attract people with backgrounds in operations research who want to pursue executive careers in business. A program in Information and Decision Sciences at the University of Illinois blends operations research, statistics, and IT, with exposure to strategy and management. At the University of Minnesota, the MBA program, which includes a concentration in information sciences, has been renamed Information and Decision Sciences. In January 2008, Johns Hopkins University chose Yash P. Gupta, a widely published operations research scholar, as the dean of the university's first and brand-new business school, the Carey School of Business. There are enough of these operations-oriented business programs to ensure that companies now have a new pool of analytic talent from which to recruit at business schools.

The Rise of the Decision Natives: Mixing It All Together

We call executives *decision natives* when they have a strong background in math and statistics, have a breadth of knowledge of business functions combined with computing technology, and are experienced leaders. Decision natives understand what decision management is all about, and they have a passion for using analytic tools to improve business processes.

Decision natives are also rare. Companies trying to compete and differentiate their business using analytics need these leaders to seed the entire organization with analytic skills. In the future, companies will need more people in executive positions who have the perspective across analytics, computing, and business operations, along with the management leadership skills to enable analytic experts and business talent to work well together.

Harrah's recruits the talent for its relationship marketing team from management consulting and consumer financial services firms.

Members of Harrah's marketing team do rotations through different business units, so that business users and analytical experts get to know each other better and work more cooperatively and proactively.

Case Study: How Harrah's Hired Decision Natives to Lead Marketing Initiatives

Gary Loveman, the CEO of Harrah's Entertainment, is a former Harvard Business School professor and math whiz who is committed to distinguishing Harrah's and maximizing customer profitability using analytics. David Norton, Harrah's senior vice-president of Relationship Marketing, is a decision native. A former American Express executive, Norton was recruited by Loveman to help lead the Harrah's strategy to become the analytic leader in the gaming industry.

A member of the company's senior executive team, Norton has built a team of more than one hundred people in the company's Customer Insight Group who oversee the management and mining of the company's rich customer database. The database is constantly refreshed through Harrah's extensive systems for interacting digitally with customers on the web and on site at the casinos. As we saw in Chapter Two, the Customer Insight Team tracks 80 percent of Harrah's revenues that are generated through its customer loyalty program, Total Rewards. The customer database fuels a mix of data-informed, data-guided, and data-driven analytics and decision management support for multiple functions—marketing, operations, customer service, and finance.

The Harrah's approach follows a hybrid structural model of a corporate function that serves business units by request. According to Forrester analyst Dave Frankland, members of the Insight team are known as "advanced marketers" rather than "analytic experts." Norton recruits the talent for the relationship marketing team from management consulting and consumer financial services firms. In his own words, Norton seeks people who "aren't too geeky and speak business language."

Norton is deliberate in weaving members of the Customer Insight team into the fabric of the organization. For example, to make sure these analytically savvy marketers don't merely field requests from business units to build simple models and run analysis, members of the marketing team do rotations through

different business units, which Norton says "demystifies 'corporate' throughout our properties" so that business users and
analytical experts get to know each other better and work more
cooperatively and proactively. The team has also built hundreds
of automated business intelligence reports so that managers
can see at least fourteen different views of customer behavior
trends geographically, seasonally, by segment, in single properties, and so on. Leaders in the business who want more detail
and a better understanding of analytic models can take a four-
day class that is taught by members of Norton's team.[9]

How Titles Signal a Company's Business Priorities

When companies have people with titles like Best Buy's vice-
president of customer insight or Harrah's senior vice-presidents
of relationship marketing, it sends a signal that customer focus
is more than mere rhetoric. Having leaders in these positions
means that decisions that affect the customer experience and
company profitability receive a high level of corporate attention
and resources. In consumer financial services, particularly retail
banks, the people who are most knowledgeable about analytic
modeling and decision management, as we define it, are usually based in risk departments. At the executive and functional
leader level, they generally hold the title of chief risk officer.

The title of *chief decision officer* is not one you will find,
although we have debates within our own company about the
merits of creating this position.

Every company has people who never go beyond the
immediate tasks for which they are responsible. Then there
are the people who have an inherent desire to run things better. Over the years, we have come across a number of decision
natives who have a passion for using data to make operational
improvements.

For example, J. P. Martin, the decision leader we introduced in Chapter Four in the Canadian Tire case study, is that kind of leader. He has spent his career in risk management working for several large consumer banks, and as long as we have known him, Martin has never been satisfied with the status quo. In a March 2008 conversation, he told us, "I always thought that if you could figure out what people buy, it would be very personal. I'd never worked for a food retailer, but I was pretty sure the difference between people who regularly buy chips and Coke versus high-quality steaks was highly predictive. I left the Royal Bank of Canada for a job at Canadian Tire in the financial services unit so I could get my hands on a richer pool of information, and have more influence over what we did with it."

Although Martin's official title at Canadian Tire was chief risk officer, unlike such positions at most financial services organizations, he was in charge of both marketing and risk. This gave his group the flexibility to dive into transaction databases owned by marketing and risk. As described in Chapter Four, the Fusion score he developed (so called because it was a scoring model that used a wide variety of data sources, not just credit bureau data) used SKU transaction data from Canadian Tire's internal databases and external merchant transaction data to model and make credit decisions. As Martin described it, "I had a bigger sandbox to play in," as he had access to a wider range of data and the latitude to be creative to make a variety of decisions based on consumer behavior. As a result, his group discovered a better predictive risk model.

Martin was informally called the chief decision officer, given his purview across marketing and risk. He thought this title reflected the innovation and leadership he brought to the role. As chief decision officer, Martin oversaw two groups:

- Decision Science: this group had one manager and seven modelers charged with building risk models and marketing models.
- Marketing Automation: this group automated marketing campaigns based on model insights.

Martin attributes the success of his unit to the versatility and talent of analysts working across marketing and risk. "You want to put together all the people that have access to the data, the warehouse, and the tools because whether you build a marketing strategy or risk strategy, the goal is the same—to book a profitable account."

How Analytics Fits Into an Organization's Structure—Or Doesn't

Although some companies have functional groups they call the analytic group, analytics does not have an obvious home in most corporations. In banks, one may find people who identify themselves as functional experts in analytics specializing in risk, marketing, or even collections. The problem is that when you assign talent to specific functions, people gain greater *functional expertise* at the expense of *analytic technical expertise* that comes if they are more functionally versatile. You can teach people who know how to create fraud models more about how to manage fraud so they understand the delicate balance of not over-identifying fraud, which could result in customer satisfaction problems if legitimate customers are mistakenly and falsely accused of fraud. This understanding of how analytics drives business results will lead to more precise and thorough fraud identification over time, but you then give up being able to leverage some of their sophisticated modeling techniques in the risk or marketing functions. When companies organize their analytic talent by functions, it encourages this kind of compartmentalization.

Overcoming Resistance to Changing Business Processes

Making improvements in business processes that require coordination among multiple functions is difficult—not only from a technology perspective but also from a human perspective.

Witness the tension between business unit leaders and CIOs, functional managers and IT managers, and down the line. Analytics is no different. Today, IT people are expected to work with statisticians and business managers and to develop the capacity to deploy analytics on top of transaction processes.

For the past thirty years, the IT department has been the champion of automating business processes. When a company is installing decision management technologies that embed analytic models in operational processes, often there is a tendency to use the old organizational model of putting IT in charge. But when you get to the "improve" stage in the decision management journey, you can't just turn these projects over to IT staff and expect to get the full benefits of the technology.

Decision management technology implementations work best when the business users, IT department, and analytic experts work together.

So who should be responsible for improving decisions? Certainly, managers in the business should have a leadership role, but most business users do not have strong backgrounds in analytics. Decision management technology implementations work best when the business users, IT department, and analytic experts work together.

The business people who own the processes have to get involved, because the operational decisions that they manage are the core of their role. Business people should sponsor and drive the cross-discipline decision management initiatives. In lending, these projects often start with the risk management and marketing department leaders. In retail, it might be the marketing or merchandising function. Where such a group exists, the customer insight function—the analytic experts—can be a bridge between the IT professionals and the business process leaders.

If a company's leader decides that he or she wants people throughout the organization to focus on improving decision making, that leader first needs to take a hard look at the company's culture and how people actually behave. Do you have the right people in place with the skills to motivate people to make improvements in decisions? Will they be creative in coming up with new solutions decisions, or are they going to be stuck in the old ways of doing things? There is always resistance when something foreign is introduced or when people feel their jobs may be in jeopardy.

One type of resistance we have found occurs in mobile phone companies, where the marketing department resists using segmentation models and predictive analytics. Marketers feel threatened that models will replace the human element of the job. As long as customers are buying their phones or signing up for their services, they figure they are doing something right. Marketing people in mobile phone companies are rainmakers, but when it stops raining because markets are more competitive and saturated, they are more willing to try something new.

Second, overt organizational resistance can also come from turf problems—that is, who owns the data? We commonly see barriers to data access that are reinforced by organizational silos, and the barriers are strong no matter whether they are business unit, product, geographic, or functional silos. The practice of analytics, especially analysis of consumer behavior, is exerting strong pressure to integrate those silos.

A third source of resistance is a bit more subtle: the business unit sees itself as running the business, not running the business *and improving* the business. So whenever there is a possibility to improve the business by changing the way it is run, business units are somewhat hesitant to act on it. For example, we talk with executives in financial services companies all the time who effectively ask us to help them improve their business processes, but at the same time they ask us to please not change anything. Operational people are so swamped by tasks that they manage in the moment. Testing and learning and experimenting are seen as a distraction to people who are tied up in the problem of the day and have finite staff and budgetary resources.

Organizing the Analytic Function

Companies organize analytic capabilities in different ways, partly because analytic professionals are a new type of talent and a new type of function. For example, we have observed analytics in consumer banks organized in one of three ways:

1. *Highly centralized.* A centralized group can look for new technologies, set standards, and cross-pollinate ideas across distributed groups.

2. *Dispersed.* In one global company that dispersed the analytic skills, the company's distributed groups were organized by region. This made sense for this company, because data was quite unique by region, and the business conditions and objectives were different by region. The analytic group can be close to the data to gather insights and close to the business leaders to ensure that their decision management solutions are relevant to the business needs.

3. *A hybrid of centralized and dispersed.* In the third type of organization, if the choice is to put analytics in a corporate function versus embedding it within individual business units, there are two natural hybrids. In the first hybrid situation, there may be a specialist in building risk models who reports to a risk manager, who has a solid line to the owner of the business unit and a dotted line to a corporate group that set credit policy. With this model, typically most of the talent is in the business units, while a small corporate group with limited staff and budget provides a high degree of value by facilitating knowledge sharing and knowledge transfer across the business units. This kind of corporate analytic group might organize events and get outside speakers and invite executives to network and share ideas. Their objective is to bring together business unit managers to talk about their strategies beyond what they are doing in their particular function and to create cohesion. For example, HSBC

Bank holds a modeling symposium once a year for its global offices.

An example of the second hybrid model is in an organization that can also take the analytic modeling function out of marketing or risk and put it together at the business unit level. No longer owned by the

> An organization can also take the analytic modeling function out of marketing or risk and put it together at the business unit level.

functions, it becomes a utility group at the business level unit that serves all the functions. This is something we are starting to see a little more frequently.

The most common structure for consumer banks varies depending on the different geographic, product, and customer segments served by the organization. Today, many banks have been based on product-centric organizational structures, so managing the customer experience first requires greater coordination and the breaking of silos. As consumer banks move toward customer-centricity, there is increasing opportunity to more effectively use analytic talent.

Moving Toward Customer-Centricity

The companies we have profiled in this book are making the journey to becoming customer-centric. We could argue that this is the most fundamental business connection that needs to be made, as organizations struggle to do cross-product analytics and customer segmentations. For example, Best Buy, Harrah's, and Tesco (all discussed in Chapter Two) made organizational changes to connect all of their internal functions that affect the customer experience. For companies that have reorganized to be more customer-centric, the challenge is to make sure they achieve the right balance between being product-centric and customer-centric. For example, when marketing and risk management decisions are coordinated across products, analytic work can be more focused on the customer experience.

Because companies from emerging market countries are building their IT infrastructures from scratch and are coming of age in economically and technologically developing countries, they are building analytic capabilities that are more advanced than many of their North American and European competitors, as the following case study illustrates.

Case Study: How India's Largest Bank Organizes Its Analytic Professionals

ICICI, the largest private-sector bank in India and the country's market leader in retail lending, is also becoming a formidable competitor internationally. ICICI has entered the U.K. market, and it has plans for further expansion in other parts of Europe and in North America where there are significant Indian immigrant populations. In India, its strategy is to understand unique local customer needs better than any of its domestic or foreign competitors and to be the employer of choice for local talent.

In 2004, ICICI's business intelligence unit of statisticians was a team of fewer than twenty-five people serving the analytic needs of the retail lending division. As of 2008, the unit has grown to over 135 people who serve all the lines of business in the bank. Johan Jarayaman, the unit's leader, calls his team "a one-stop shop analytics group". As shown in Figure 5.1, this group provides a spectrum of support to the businesses, from the low-end management reporting, which is less complex and less valuable, to the high-end decision management capabilities like predictive modeling and optimization, which are more complex yet add more value. There is value in combining these functions, as they share data assets. In Chapter Seven, we look at the future of decision management and analytics and how emerging market giants such as India's ICICI and Turkey's Akbank are leading the way.

Figure 5.1   ICICI's Decision and Analytic Tools

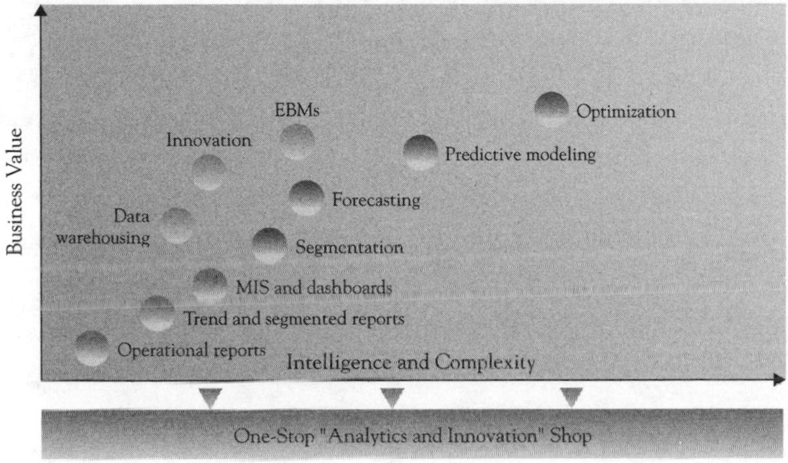

Source: ICICI Bank

Conclusion: What Are the Optimal People Strategies?

Companies need data geeks to perform the analysis, but they also need them to be able to put the output of analytics into a *business* perspective. Companies need business leaders who may not be expert in both math and business strategy but have an appreciation for both. In the past, statisticians did not work closely with business managers. Now it is a necessity that the MBAs and the mathematicians get together.

Sometimes people with technical skills who have a head for business want to take on leadership roles outside the analytic functions. For example, we knew a branch manager of a sales team for a bank who spent a lot of time getting to understand the analytic technology. He could not build the models, but he knew when the math mattered and when it didn't. On both technical and managerial career tracks, you can find people who are passionate about using math to solve business problems and who make unexpected contributions. When decision natives join the senior management team, it is a sign that the organization has recognized analytics as a competitive resource. Few companies have decision natives in leadership positions today, but more will in the future, particularly as these highly transferrable skills can take advantage of a foundational set of technologies—such as predictive models, descriptive segmentation models, and decision models—that have now been proven to deliver results when applied to a variety of business problems across multiple industries.

6

DEMYSTIFYING DECISION MANAGEMENT

A Primer on Various Analytic Tools and Techniques

In their bestselling book *Freakonomics*, authors Steven Levitt and Stephen Dubner wrote, "If you can learn to look at data in the right way, you can explain riddles that might otherwise have seemed impossible. Because there is nothing like the power of numbers to scrub away layers of confusion and contradiction."[1]

Indeed, by mining multiple databases and asking cunning questions, Levitt, the rogue economist, explained dozens of confounding riddles (for example, why the decisions and actions of one woman living in Dallas, Texas, in 1970 led to a massive drop in crime in the United States in the 1990s). There were surprises, too (for example, the propensity of teachers to cheat).

Some dismal scientists question the seriousness of Levitt's freakonomics, but no one is debating the value of scrubbing the data to find *more useful information*—that's exactly our goal in our work at Fair Isaac and in this book. The algorithmic techniques Fair Isaac has used for years to predict credit behavior are spawning a "new breed of number crunchers" in other consumer industries, as Yale law professor Ian Ayers calls them in his popular book about data mining, *Super Crunchers: Why Thinking-by-the-Numbers Is the New Way to Be Smart*.

Indeed, the digital age has never been a better time to be a business professional with a mind for mathematics. As described in Chapter Five, we see more and more companies adding people with advanced math and computer modeling skills to their marketing teams to gain competitive advantage by using their customer data more effectively: MBAs are being paired with people who have master's degrees and Ph.D.s in mathematics, statistics, and computer science. In these visionary companies, decision management is a business approach that pulls together the know-how of mathematicians, information technologists, and executives, managers, and employees.

But as we explain in this chapter, the analytics and math are only one part of a bigger story of decision management that we want to tell. Decision management also relates to a class of information technology that automates, improves, and connects decisions in one or many business processes throughout an enterprise. In this chapter, we illustrate how there's an entire spectrum of decision making; we clarify the difference between *decision flow* and *work flow*. We also clarify the difference between *descriptive* analytics, *predictive* analytics, and *decision* analytics—and we show how each type can help your company in different ways, drawing on case studies from our own FICO® score as well as ING Financial Services and Google. Finally, we conclude the chapter by clarifying the difference between *decision management* and ordinary, everyday *business intelligence*—because they're not the same thing at all.

Decision Management Unlocks Value in Data

The Internet, e-mail, data warehouses, radio frequency identification technology (RFID), enterprise resource planning (ERP) software, iPods, cell phones—virtually any technology that stores digital information—are all repositories of potentially valuable data. The challenge for corporations has been to do a better job of creating business value from data, because many have overinvested in the technology to store and collect data without investing in the key automated analytic capabilities to apply the data to decision management. As Gartner, Inc., analyst

Figure 6.1   The "Execution Gap" Between the Data a Typical Company Has and What It Can Actually Use

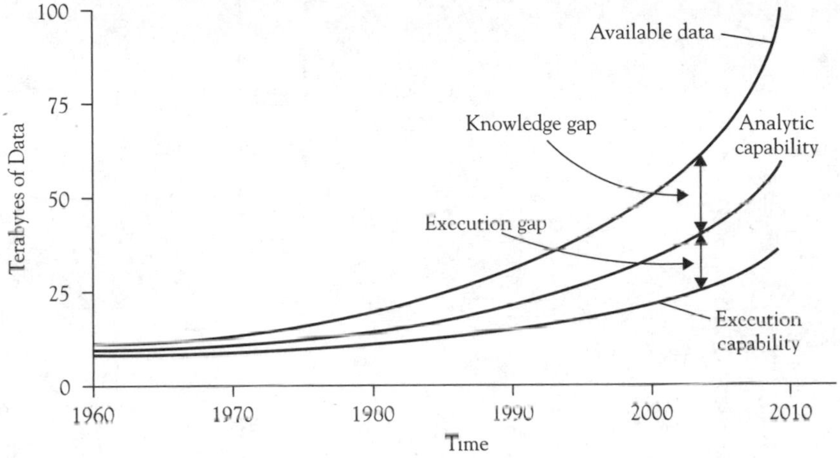

Source: "CRM Analytics and the Integration of Insight," Gareth Herschel presentation at the Customer Relationship Management Summit, Gartner, Inc., London, March 7–8, 2007.

Gareth Herschel shows in Figure 6.1, most corporations' ability to *collect* data is increasing faster than the ability to *use* the data.

Decision management is a path to close that execution gap. Decision management unlocks data in functional silos (see Figure 6.2) and creates a unified system that creates a *critical feedback loop between data and actions.* As we will explain later in the chapter, what distinguishes decision management systems from other types of decision support is that these systems incorporate predictive analytic models and use those predictions to automate decisions all the way through to an operational action being taken.

Data from external and internal sources forms the raw material that companies use to perform analytics. Analytics finds meaning in data through the discovery of patterns and relationships among the data. Different types of analytic models provide the input to make better decisions. Sometimes analytic models simply augment an expert judgment. Other times they are part of an automated system that executes decisions. Automated systems often handle

Figure 6.2   Creating a Feedback Loop from the Traditional Silo Components of Decision Management

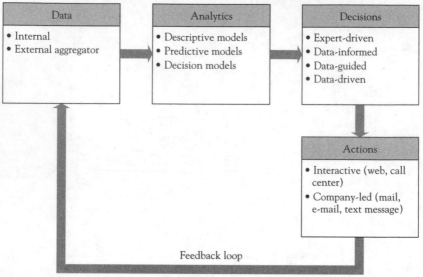

Company actions + Customer reactions = Results

Source: Fair Isaac

high-volume decision making in real time. For example, credit card authorization decisions result in 'approve' or 'decline' actions that occur at the point of sale, and they are fully automated, data-driven decisions supported by complex analytics.

Where Is Your Company on the Spectrum of Decision Making?

We use a "decision taxonomy" to present the spectrum of decision making, from expert-driven (where there's pure judgment, but no analytics used) to data-driven (which relies purely on analytics and is fully automated):

- *Expert-driven.* There is no math or analytics involved. This is purely empirical judgment based on expertise and experience. For example, banks that are expanding into new countries will initially lack data to evaluate loan applications, but they can use their experience from other countries to identify important lending criteria such as income and occupation and request that information on loan applications.

- *Data-informed*. Data-informed decision making relies on the expert to interpret information that is provided in report form to improve the expert's own decision making. For example, a manager may look at a report of branch performance for banks in a large region in order to decide on staffing levels and product promotions at each branch.

- *Data-guided*. This is where, for example, a predictive analytic model replaces unproven assumptions with objective information. Analytic models may provide one or more advisory decisions that the expert can choose or override. For example, a call center agent may receive a prompt from their computer system to cross-sell one of three potential offers to a given customer. Those offers may be based on a model that predicts the likelihood of a customer accepting the offer, but this is a guided decision in that the agent can use their judgment to select from, or even to ignore the offer if the customer on the line happens to be having a negative customer service experience.

- *Data-driven*. The running of analytic models and execution of decisions are completely automated. For example, activating a cell phone occurs in real time, as there is a data-driven process that automatically approves customers with a credit score above a specified level, so they can begin using their cell phones from the moment they purchase them. Some systems are designed with a manual review process to allow an expert to override automated decisions under some circumstances; for example, a transaction may be flagged as potentially fraudulent, but the transaction may still be approved if it is for a high-value customer purchasing an essential item such as gasoline.

Business rules management software captures the logic used to automate specific decisions and actions for specific consumers. The simplest form of a business rule is "if this, then that" or "if this, don't do that." For example:

- If a customer spends more than $200 at a website, you send them an e-mail with a 10-percent-off coupon for the customer's next purchase.

- Customers who spend more than $25 get free shipping, whereas customers who spend less pay full shipping fees.

The Next Wave of Automation Using Decision Management

Analytic professionals who build models and the business decision makers who use the models work together to define the business rules. These are decision strategies designed through the use of data and expert judgment. Rules can be applied across business functions and processes, and they can be changed as often and as fast as business conditions require. This class of software is also "decision neutral"—you can set it up for any kind of decision or process, from approving claims to running a robot. Sophisticated math embedded in analytic software can automate millions of operational decisions.

However, automation in decision management does not mean organizations are relying less on the experience and expertise of human beings. In fact, decision management technologies all involve, to different degrees, human inputs and data insights. There is significant math and creativity that goes into creating decision models; choosing the variables to construct a model is an art and a science.

Most companies have reached the limits of wringing costs out of business processes through automation of nonstrategic administrative business processes (such as payroll and employee benefits administration, receivables management). This started back in the 1970s, led by the IT department. When reengineering hit in the 1990s, once again IT led the cost-reduction crusade to automate or outsource whole processes. We think the next wave of automation using decision management will be to improve and connect decisions to achieve competitive differentiation and revenue growth. This is especially critical in mass-market consumer businesses that are trying to lower the cost of differentiating their products and services by delivering unique value to customers that competitors can't match.

Automating *Decision Flow* Is Different from Automating *Work Flow*

Think of a business process as having two elements: a *work flow* and a *decision flow*. A work flow is a well-defined set of actions associated with an operational task. A decision flow is the set of alternatives or choices made in the given work flow. For example, suppose your business process is the direct mail marketing of credit cards to new customers. The decision flow that relates to this business process includes many decisions, such as these:

- What products and product features you should offer
- Which prospective customers you should target
- When to send offers to these people
- Which channels you should use to send your offers

The first era of business process automation addressed work flows. Decision management is intended to address the effectiveness of *decision flows*. But the goal of improving the business process is the same: to obtain more value each time the process is executed.

Decision management is not a capability a company can develop quickly or easily, as we saw in Chapter Four. Because in the first era of big corporate IT the investments were made in data collection and storage, companies are only now beginning to grasp the concept of creating systems to manage decision flows. Furthermore, decision management requires sharing data and coordinating decisions, and for most companies this is difficult because data is locked in functional silos. For example, in a bank there may be eight or more such silos:

- Marketing
- Product management
- Credit risk
- Finance
- Collections
- Customer service
- Operations
- Compliance

Furthermore, marketing, risk, and operations are often split into account acquisition and account management. The functional silos are common in every industry. Although process reengineering of workflows and applications of enterprise software have helped to achieve basic integration of the functional silos present in most businesses, most businesses have failed to take the next step of integrating technology to improve decision flow among functions. This is required to reach the next level of benefit of decision management.

A Primer on Analytic Techniques

Descriptive analytics looks for and describes relationships among data, without ascribing meaning to the patterns. Descriptive analytics is more exploratory than prescriptive.

Companies that use analytic tools may or may not think of analytics in the context of managing decisions. But if you do think of the framework we just described, analytics are the heart of decision management. Some models are developed to make predictions. Some discover and describe patterns. Some use predictions and descriptions to make decisions. Let's look at each type in the following sections.

Using *Descriptive Analytics* to Understand Your Customers' Past Behavior and Interests

Traditional consumer market research starts with demographic and psychographic categorizations to see what customers in different categories should be interested in purchasing. However, you can drill down even more specifically and segment or classify large groups of people who share similar characteristics by using *descriptive analytics*, which will help your company develop marketing strategies based on the particular interests and behaviors of these groups.

This type of analytics looks for, and describes, *relationships among data*, without ascribing meaning to the patterns. Descriptive analytics is more *exploratory* than *prescriptive*. It is a way to talk about the *past and current* behaviors and interests of your customers (or your prospective customers) with no particular sense of a *future* response in mind. For example, a client might come to us and say, "I know all my customers are not the same, but I don't know how to talk to them separately; I need to group them in some intelligent way." As we discussed in Chapter Two, this is how Best Buy used customer segment representatives such as Barry, Buzz, and Jill to reach higher levels of growth.

> *Descriptive analytics is a way to talk about the* past and current *behaviors and interests of your customers (or your* prospective customers), with *no particular sense of a* future *response in mind.*

There are countless ways to use descriptive models, and that is part of the art and science for marketers to figure out, based on their company's business goals. For example, two companies might find that 20 percent of their customers are women who own minivans and have several kids. One company might say, "That's great to know, except we don't want to market to these people, so find out other things about these mothers that we care about." The other company is interested and wants to know how to market to them, but these are not decisions that descriptive analytics can prescribe. This shortfall is addressed by *predictive analytics*, a technique that we explain later in this chapter.

Retail market basket analysis is another kind of descriptive analytics. Retailers try to figure out what groups of products consumers are going to buy *together* when they go to the store, so the retailer can determine where it should place the product in the store, or whether it should discount things together (such as with a "buy one, get one free" promotion). For example, supermarkets offer pastas in the same aisle as pasta sauces; electronics stores offer high-end video gaming PCs along with joysticks and software—because these products go together so obviously. Often the merchandisers make these placement or promotion decisions while considering the typical and highest-profit market baskets. Here the application is not trying to group *customers* together; rather, it is trying to group *transactions* and *products* together to find some pattern.

Although in the past segmentation analysis began and ended in the marketing department, now we have the technology to automate the execution of decisions across a complex operating environment. It was traditionally easy for mass marketers to make their decisions based on segments, because all they had to do was send a predefined set of offers to specific customer groups. This was one-time, one-way communication. Fortunately, with the advent of the Internet and other two-way channels, vastly refined segmentation—which has gone from the basic two segments to millions of segments, one for each customer—is becoming more important to operations so that your customers receive differentiated treatment across different points of interaction with your company. This has placed added pressure on marketers to find the right balance in segmentation—so that it's *personalized* enough to be perceived as "individual" by the customer yet *broad* enough so that operations can achieve profitable operating levels. If it is too broad, then your customers will get turned off; if it's too personalized, then your company's operations may become so complex that it will not be cost effective.

> *Predictive analytics is the practice of relating what you* do *know at the time you make a decision to what you* don't *know: what might happen in the future.*

Using *Predictive Analytics* to Determine Possible Outcomes from a Contemplated Decision

Predictive analytics is the practice of relating what you *do* know at the time you make a decision to what you *don't* know: what might happen in the future. Whereas descriptive analytics *describes* patterns, predictive analytics *ascribes meaning to* those patterns. Using a variety of statistical, computing, and mathematical techniques, consumer businesses use predictive analytics to find behavioral patterns in historical consumer data that forecast the likelihood of a particular outcome.

Case Study: Using the FICO Score to Predict a Customer's Credit-Worthiness

The credit score is a classic example of predictive analytics. FICO scores provide a reliable guide to lending risk, based solely on data from credit bureaus. The FICO score is calculated through an algorithm that takes into account multiple variables and then expresses the score as one number in the 300 to 850 range. The higher the score, the less risk a borrower is to a creditor. Scores are based on variables such as these:

- How often a person has applied for credit
- How much credit that person has outstanding (that is, not paid)

- The customer's repayment record
- The kinds of loans the customer has—such as a mortgage, a car loan, or a student loan

The basic idea behind any credit scoring algorithm is to choose and weight a set of predictive variables that offer a forecast of a person's likelihood to manage debts responsibly based on the person's past actions.

Predictive analytics express the future in terms of odds or probabilities; that is, people with these behavioral characteristics have a one in five chance of defaulting on a loan. For example, if you go to www.myfico.com, you can see how different FICO scores affect a person's interest rates and payments for a loan: as our tag line on the website says, "The higher your FICO credit score, the lower your payments!" See Exhibit 6.1.

"Complexity in the science, simplicity in the solution" is a phrase that has been floating around Fair Isaac for a long time. It's attributed to Pat Culhane, a former Fair Isaac executive who helped build the credit bureau risk-scoring business. A single score guides millions of credit decisions every day. Although calculating scores is a complex process, the actual score—that is, whether a prospective customer has a 480 FICO score or a 720 FICO score—is something companies and consumers can easily understand. Credit bureau scoring is also a classic example of how automation can be used to deploy an analytic model to improve the scale and speed of decision making and the quality of decisions.

Although calculating scores is a complex process, the actual score—that is, whether a prospective customer has a 480 or a 720 FICO score—is something companies and consumers can easily understand.

These predictive models are mathematically precise, but they can't perfectly predict the behavior

Exhibit 6.1   Interactive FICO Score Interest Rate Calculator from MyFICO.com

The higher your FICO® credit score, the lower your payments!

See for yourself. Interest rates accurate as of September 16, 2008:

30 Year fixed mortgage		
FICO® score	APR	Monthly payment *
760–850	5.631%	$1,728
700–759	5.853%	$1,770
660–699	6.137%	$1,825
620–659	6.947%	$1,985
580–619	9.451%	$2,512
500–579	10.310%	$2,702

Location| National Avg. ▾ | Loan amount | $300,000 | *Estimated average over the life of the loan. Payments may vary.

of an individual consumer. No score can say for sure whether a specific individual will pay as agreed or not. And although many banks and insurers use FICO scores to help them make decisions about how to treat different customers, each company has its own strategy, including the "cutoff score" or level of acceptable risk for a given product and a given person. For example, referring back to Exhibit 6.1, you'll note that although the low end of the FICO scoring system is actually 300, the interactive chart begins with a still relatively low score of 500—that's because most banks and mortgage lenders won't lend money to potential customers who have a credit score lower than 500.

Another former Fair Isaac colleague, Mort Schwartz, used to say that if an individual credit officer makes three loans to lion tamers that all go bad, that credit officer will probably not lend to lion tamers again. However, the lending organization's experience with *hundreds or thousands* of lion tamers (instead of only three) may be quite different. Human minds organize such qualitative experiential feedback to improve their decision making. The beauty of credit scoring—and computer-based analytical tools like it—is that an entire organization can accumulate and process the experience from vast amounts of data to make quantitative objective decisions on an enterprise level.

Case Study: How ING Financial Used Predictive Analytics to Reduce the Costs of Its Claims Management Process

Predictive models are being used in many different ways as valuable tools for improving business processes through automation. For example, ING, a Dutch insurance company, installed a decision automation system based on predictive analysis to lower the cost of its benefits claims management process while speeding up service. ING was using a screen for fraudulent claims that was slowing down the claims process for customers and not detecting significant fraud. So the company implemented a real-time system to analyze claims to identify those that were unlikely to be fraudulent. Based on proprietary analysis (which we therefore can't share with you in this book) of the factors that indicated a fraudulent or nonfraudulent claim, ING was able to identify the claims that could be settled without a screen.

The result? This new system raised customer satisfaction as payments were made more quickly, and it reduced processing costs by 20 to 40 percent over the previous claims management process, with only a small increase in losses due to fraud. In this case, ING systematically identified a way to shorten claim processing for select customers. Here, predictive analytics offered a one-two punch: a better way to manage resource constraints (that is, costs) and greater customer satisfaction.

Case Study: How Google Used Predictive Analytics to Streamline Its Hiring Process

Google celebrated its tenth year in 2008, and the company is still receiving more than a hundred thousand job applications a month. From that pool, it aims to hire approximately eight hundred people per month—a volume that doubles the company's size in a single year. To be able to find the best candidates and meet its growth goals, Google developed a predictive algorithm to screen and select applications before the interview process began. "As we get bigger, we find it harder and harder to find enough people," said Laszlo Bock, Google's vice-president for people operations. "With traditional hiring methods, we were worried we will overlook some of the best candidates . . . Interviews are a terrible predictor of performance."[?]

The underlying analytics for the new Google recruiting tool is scoring. To create the model, the company surveyed current employees to build a database of current employee traits and characteristics. The survey asked employees to provide a variety of information, including biographical details, successes and failures working in teams, formative experiences (such as having been a tutor in high school), and outstanding accomplishments (such as starting an organization before the age of twenty).

Next, the company statistically determined the characteristics and traits of top performers and differentiated them from low-performing and average employees.

Then Google created the algorithm to analyze candidate applications and give a score from 0 to 100. Most applicants have the intellectual credentials; the score is meant to predict whether the person can perform and fit in Google's unique culture and work environment. John Sullivan, the former chief talent officer at Agilent Technologies (a forty-three-thousand-employee Hewlett-Packard spin-off), admires Google's decision to not just be data-driven but to also look for atypical data. The algorithm evaluates a much wider range of potential success predictors than the typical ones (grades, SAT scores, Ivy League degrees). "Although many companies seek to screen out candidates, the new Google candidate assessment approach enables Google to 'include' candidates that might otherwise be overlooked."[3]

Scoring is a compensatory mechanism. As the Google model shows, a person may score low on one or more characteristics but score well enough on others to more than compensate for the low scores. For example, Larry participated in a nonprofit working group to develop predictive algorithms to help businesses find high-potential employees among high school dropouts whom they would otherwise ignore. If a job description containing "High-school diploma required" is a hard-and-fast decision rule, people who haven't finished high school usually can't even get an interview to reveal other strengths. Perhaps someone

Google was receiving a hundred thousand job applications every month, so it created an algorithm to automate the review process. Each applicant's score was meant to predict how well that person would fit with Google's unique culture and work environment.

was raised by a single parent and had to drop out of high school to work to put food on the table for his family, or had to stay home when his mother became ill.

Employers know the presence of a high-school diploma is a poor proxy for the qualities they are looking for in a new hire, but they also know that high school dropouts, as a subpopulation, are very risky to hire—and employers don't have the tools to efficiently assess and rank order those risks. As a result, they often stick with the "diploma required" rule, even though they can train dropouts to become successful employees. Just as credit scoring has helped millions of more people qualify for credit, predictive analytics applied in this situation could help millions of people get a job.

Summing Up the Benefits of Predictive Analytics

Predictive analytics is a powerful tool to manage high-volume decisions in near or real time. These predictive models swing into action to analyze billions of historical datapoints and transactions to isolate patterns and characteristics. Predictive analytics have become especially sophisticated in applications to help companies anticipate the behaviors of customers that are on the verge of defecting, so that companies can take some action to prevent this from happening if a customer is one they want to keep.

> Predictive analytics is a powerful tool to manage high-volume decisions in near or real time: it analyzes billions of historical datapoints and transactions to isolate patterns and characteristics.

Fair Isaac's fraud-detection product has eliminated billions of dollars of credit card fraud over the past two decades. By feeding in the most recent cases of fraudulent and nonfraudulent transactions, a company can retrain a neural network model to detect the latest patterns in fraud when predictions and decisions must be made in a split second of real time. There was a time when companies simply wrote off losses from fraud and accepted it as a cost of doing business. No more. These systems save companies managing millions of transactions every day, involving multi-millions of dollars every year.

Fair Isaac's fraud-detection product has eliminated billions of dollars of credit card fraud over the past two decades.

Mathematically precise though the models may be, it is impossible to be sure that the assumptions used in them will be perfect or that the models themselves will be used to make good decisions. As twentieth-century mathematician Kurt Gödel said, "Mathematics is perfect. But it is not complete." Incompleteness in a credit score might happen because the score is calculated from inaccurate credit report data or because it does not contain important variables due to gaps in historical data.

Using Decision Analytics to Predict the Outcomes of Complex Business Decisions

Decision modeling is the most advanced form of business analytics. Decision models predict the outcomes of complex decisions for a business in much the same way that predictive models are used to predict consumer behavior. In Chapter Four we explored the use of adaptive control to test new operating points for credit limits, and those tests can be conducted with a focus on a few select variables, such as credit losses, without knowing the precise impact of several variables when considered together. The decision model first maps the relationships between all the elements of a decision:

- The known data
- The decision you're considering making
- The forecasted results of the decision (including results of predictive models)

The decision model predicts what will happen to your bottom-line profit if a given action is taken. You can then use these models to improve your business's performance by deriving decision strategies that find more favorable trade-offs among your company's key business objectives (for example, if your goal is to maximize revenue growth) while minimizing losses and expenses. Optimization is a mathematical process to find the best decision model strategy for a given business problem. Decision models are generally used to create decision strategies and business rules that are then automated via application software.

For instance, credit card issuers use decision models to determine how large a credit line increase, if any, they should offer to different groups of credit card holders. A mathematical model of the decision links the quantitative relationships among four types of elements:

- The data elements we know about the prospects or customers at the time of the decision—in this example, the card-holders' risk scores, their current balance and limit, recent spending activities, and finance charges assessed

- The decision to be made—in this case, the amount of a credit line increase (which could be zero) to give to each cardholder

- The consumer's behavioral reactions to the decision made and the action taken—for instance, how much more spending, balance building, and incremental repayment risk will occur as a result of giving the consumer this credit line increase

- The impact of those behavior reactions on the credit card issuer's key business metrics—in this example, incremental revenue, receivable balance, credit loss, and profit contribution

Having constructed a formal mathematical model, the lender can, in theory, solve for the optimal credit line increase to give to each cardholder, based on known objectives, constraints, decision variables, and data at any given time. But when growth in revenues and receivables is the dominant objective, the optimal credit line increases will be very different from increases in times of caution when the bank seeks profit increases with zero increases in credit losses.

The business value of a well-crafted decision model is twofold:

1. First, you can map out a sharper picture of your choices, and you can do so in quantitative terms.

2. Second, you can more easily see which choices will result in more favorable trade-offs among your company's key business metrics: in other words, your choices are more visible.

These decision models are able to take complete departmental processes and objectives and represent them with mathematics. In turn, this enables managers to more easily see precise trade-offs between the primary business metrics of one department and another, such as the loss metric of the risk management department versus the volume metric of the marketing department—as we described in Chapter Four, in the discussion of how Dell Financial Services handled this exact problem—or the loss metric of the risk management department versus the profit contribution of the finance department.

Decision Management Is Not Business Intelligence

Historically, when investing in information technology, business executives and IT professionals have not delineated between products and systems used for collection and storage, processing and reporting, and decision management. This is not surprising, given that, for decades, the costs and complexity of collecting and storing data were so high. In fact, vendors themselves have not made these distinctions clear either.

Even today, vendors and the IT media often use the terms *business intelligence* (BI) and *analytics* interchangeably, and often indiscriminately, to describe the functions of such products as business dashboard reporting, which enable managers to take a step back from the details and view their business through visually rich elements such as gauges, maps, and charts. Hundreds of different BI tools, offered by hundreds of different vendors, present data to business managers in these forms, which are easy for them to manipulate and use to make high-level decisions.

Although BI is an important category of business software that provides significant value in the form of decision support, it is different from decision management, as shown in Figure 6.3. BI products typically report *past* business performance or a *current* condition. Reports track macro trends, and the data presented is used as either background or affirmation for a decision a manager makes, but the BI tools themselves do not automate decisions based on predictive or descriptive models that trigger actions.

For example, a regional manager of a national consumer bank—we'll call him Bob—uses a business intelligence dashboard to monitor the volume and sales of different lending and

Figure 6.3   How Business Intelligence Differs from Decision Management

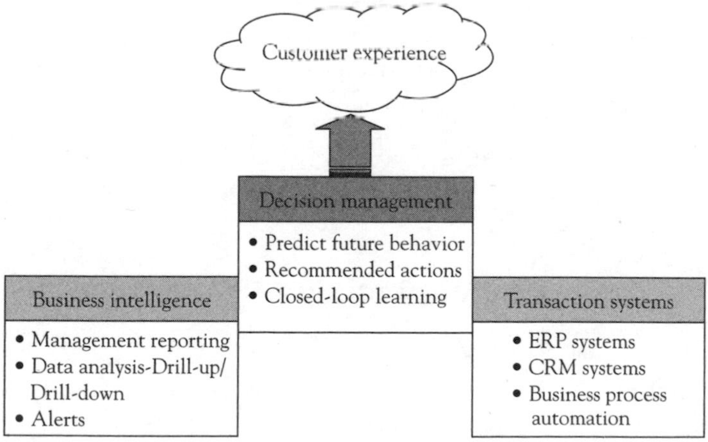

demand deposit products at the branch level. Lending products may include credit cards, mortgages, auto loans, and small business loans; demand deposits are savings accounts, checking accounts, and debit cards. The number of products multiplied by the number of branches makes for a complex business, but in looking at a report, Bob notices that demand deposit volume is falling sharply in Miami, although growth in the product line in the rest of the state is strong. Bob calls several other branch managers in Miami and finds out the cause of the problem in his region: a competitor is running a free-checking promotion. The dashboard has analyzed a cause and an effect, but it has not made any decisions, and it does not take action. Should Bob's bank launch its own free-checking promotion? If it does, how should the bank market it? And to *all* customers or to only *select* customers?

As you can see from this example, BI *overlaps* with data management, and it adds aggregated reporting, but it *does not* make decisions. Predictive and descriptive analytic models determine, based on the data, whether free checking targeted to a select population will substantially lower the cost of the promotion, attract more profitable prospects, and aid branch managers in their efforts to interest existing customers in other products. Although business intelligence and decision management are different, both are important technologies. The biggest risk for business is failing to recognize the difference, which has led some businesses to invest only in data and business intelligence to create informative reports on market trends or anomalies. But this limited approach fails to connect the "last mile" of decision management: connecting analytic insights on consumer behavior and interactions to decisions and actions.

Competing on Decision Management

In a recent issue of the *Harvard Business Review,* MIT professors Andrew McAfee and Erik Brynjolfsson presented the results of a two-year study that looked at the connection between IT investments and competitiveness (as opposed to the connection between human productivity and IT investment, which has been studied more closely). The study evaluated the financial performance of public U.S. companies in all industries from the 1960s to 2005. They found that the spread between the highest and lowest performers in terms of sales, earnings, profitability, and market capitalization has been widening since 1995—the same period in which companies began to change their existing operating models to take advantage of the Internet and enterprise software.[4]

Brynjolfsson and McAfee are not the only business strategy thought leaders who are seeing the link between innovations in technology and corporate competitiveness and innovation. In their book *The New Age of Innovation*, management scholar and strategist C. K. Prahalad and M. S. Krishnan, a professor of information technology, present the building blocks of an IT architecture in four layers, as shown in Figure 6.4.

Figure 6.4   The Building Blocks of IT Architecture

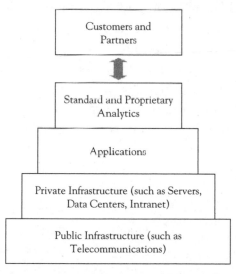

Source: Adapted with permission from C. K. Prahalad and M. S. Krishnan, *The New Age of Innovation: Driving Co-Created Value Through Global Networks* (McGraw-Hill, 2008), Figure 2.2, 54.

Their diagram makes a powerful point that company differentiation and competitive advantage are moving to the analytic layer. This is because it is quickly becoming the only layer that is unique for a company; all other layers have become standardized and commoditized. It is also becoming the interface layer between company and consumer.

Company differentiation and competitive advantage are moving to the analytic layer . . . all other layers have become standardized and commoditized.

One could argue that the bottom layer became a commodity when the Internet took off in the 1990s. In parallel, during the 1980s and 1990s, companies were building sophisticated private networks as a source of differentiation (for example, FedEx, Wal-Mart, Visa), but there have not been any new companies in this category for more than ten years. In the 1990s and into the early 2000s, differentiation moved to the applications layer, but as companies have standardized on enterprise software systems from dominant ERP vendors such as SAP, Oracle/Siebel, and the like, competitive advantage in this area has waned. The future of differentiation and innovation lies in analytics and, we would add, decision management.

As technology and mathematics experts work more closely with executives to use data to conceive innovative business models and make business processes more competitive, the underlying analytics and decision management technology will become less mysterious. And the opportunities to use these resources for competitive advantage will become more apparent. As IT infrastructures become streamlined and integrated, it will be easier to automate analysis and decision making and to use information technology and managerial leadership to elevate the quality of strategic and tactical decision making throughout enterprises.

Technology is no substitute for a strong leader who promotes smarter decision making everywhere in his or her company, but it can make a great strategy even greater.

Of course, technology is no substitute for a strong leader who promotes smarter decision making everywhere in his or her company, but it can make a great strategy even greater. For example, in his management memoir, *Jack: Straight from the Gut*, Jack Welch reflected on what strategy meant to him during his years leading GE: "Business strategy is less a function of grandiose predictions than it is a result of being able to respond rapidly to real changes as they occur. That's why strategy has to be dynamic and anticipatory . . . . Strategy was not a lengthy action plan. It was the execution of a single idea through continually changing circumstances."[5]

At GE, Welch was able to link strategy to execution through cultural underpinnings such as a disciplined management style, a focus on a few big ideas (for example, GE needs to be number one or number two in any market), a common management methodology (Six Sigma), and a comprehensive management training program. Welch's cultural approach was to ensure that decisions made throughout the company and on the front line were executed in a way consistent with the company's strategy.

The unique charisma and drive that Welch used to create a culture of execution at GE is not something that can be replicated. But many aspects of the focus on execution that Welch reinforced through culture and management programs (such as Six Sigma) can be similarly developed and reinforced using decision management technology systems—for example:

- *Predictive analytics* gives business the "anticipatory" capabilities Welch highlighted.
- *Rules management software* gives businesses the ability to change decisions and execution as the strategy changes (that is, rapid response).
- *Decision models and optimization* enable businesses to balance competing and conflicting objectives.

- *Data- and analytic-driven customer segmentation* is another way to bridge strategy and execution: it enables businesses to operate efficiently and at the same time treat customers in a way that may feel personal to them.

Conclusion: Putting All the Pieces Together

Some companies have great data warehouses. Others use the reporting piece of business intelligence to great effect. But to do decision management well, you need to ensure that *all* of the components—the data, the analytics, the decisions, and the actions—*work together* and fit *your* business needs.

> Decision management infuses intelligence into your business processes, thereby providing a source of value creation that can propel your business to stand alone in the marketplace.

Companies should use a variety of analytic techniques, with different levels of sophistication, depending on the business problem. If your company is using decision management to become more customer-centric, the analytics must tie into your operations so you are making decisions and taking actions that affect consumer behavior and profitability in a positive direction while creating competitive advantage.

You can achieve business process improvements without differentiating your company in the marketplace. However, at its best, decision management infuses intelligence into your business processes, thereby providing a source of value creation that can propel your business to stand alone in the marketplace and in the eyes of each and every one of your customers.

With this in mind, Chapter Seven looks at the *future* of decision management and how your company will be able to use your data to even greater advantage than you can now.

7

THE FUTURE OF DECISION MANAGEMENT

Using Differentiated Decisions to Gain Competitive Advantage

Throughout this book, we argue that corporate success is becoming more dependent on millions, even billions, of operational decisions. How can you and other managers deal with the growing complexity of your business and meet the needs of more demanding consumers? How can you use bountiful data more effectively to differentiate your products and services from your competition's and increase your competitive advantage? How can your company make better use of data and computing technology to increase your managerial productivity and creativity?

These are the challenges and questions that will make decision management a vital business discipline in the future. One could argue that decision management is the missing link between strategy and execution. But the issue is more than linking strategy and execution; it's about integrating multiple strategies. This is how Chuck Lucier, a strategy consultant who was a senior partner at Booz Allen Hamilton (now Booz & Co.), describes it:

> "Great strategy, poor execution" is, in fact, a pernicious oxymoron, rooted in ineffective concepts that sharply separate the formulation of strategy from its execution, and assume that there is a linear, sequential relationship between the two . . . Although business gurus have documented the inadequacy of the linear

"strategy-first-execution-next" view in today's business environment, no one has provided businesspeople with actionable concepts they can use to replace the old thinking. A new framework
is needed—one that views strategy as an integrated change program linking together multiple dimensions of strategy: external
realities, internal activities and business processes, financial targets, and customers. We think of this as "integrated strategy."[1]

We think decision management is the crucial link to the
successful execution of integrated strategy. Many of the best
generals of the twentieth century have been those who bring
the strategy into the field. As Dwight D. Eisenhower said, "Plans
are nothing, planning is everything." Things happen on the
battlefield that no one anticipates, but the better prepared
the troops, the more likely they are to complete their mission.
If defining a vision and mission is the process to set a course
for the corporation, decision management is the process that
enables employees to bring the strategy into the field.

The tools and resources to perform decision management
are accessible to people throughout a company, and they keep
evolving and improving. Data sources to describe and predict
consumer behavior are growing fast in volume, variety, and
value. The technology to embed analytical decision logic in corporate computing systems is getting better, and it is in the hands
of a more capable workforce. In this environment, analytics
and decision management generate business process improvements that are continuous and rapid and that drive corporate
competitiveness.

This final chapter describes five
key business trends affecting the
use of analytic tools and decision
management, with examples from
Air Products, Facebook, General
Motors, Procter & Gamble, Macy's,
Microsoft, Google, MasterCard,

> If defining a vision and mission is the process to set a course for the corporation, decision management is the process that enables employees to bring the strategy into the field.

and two of the rising stars in retail banking in emerging markets, Akbank (Turkey's largest retail bank) and ICICI (India's second largest retail bank). The chapter wraps up by describing how things are changing in the three consumer industries we think are going to be setting the standards for excellence decision management over the next five years: financial services, health care, and retail.

How Decision Management Delivers Differentiation

Today's enterprise resource planning (ERP) software platform systems have not been around long—SAP's ERP platform was introduced in 1992—but the technology has had a transformative effect on corporate operations. This first wave of enterprise IT has been very effective at reducing costs to increase profits. The next wave is one of better decision processes that lead to differentiation that matters to customers and drives revenue growth. Some may view this statement as just another customer relationship management (CRM) maneuver, but the difference is that analytics and decision management can deliver what CRM has not.

For example, let's take another look at the "Building Blocks of IT Architecture" we introduced in Chapter Six, with some modifications. Figure 7.1 shows how the components of decision management drive differentiation.

- At *the private infrastructure layer,* most businesses have robust servers, networks, and database software that are on a par with their competitors. Decision-based differentiation occurs at this layer when data is carefully selected and stored so that it is available to the application software that makes decisions in real time, and it makes data available to analysts to improve decision making over time.

- At *the applications layer,* there is a new source of competitive advantage: specifically, from software to manage decision

Figure 7.1   Building Differentiation Through Decision Management

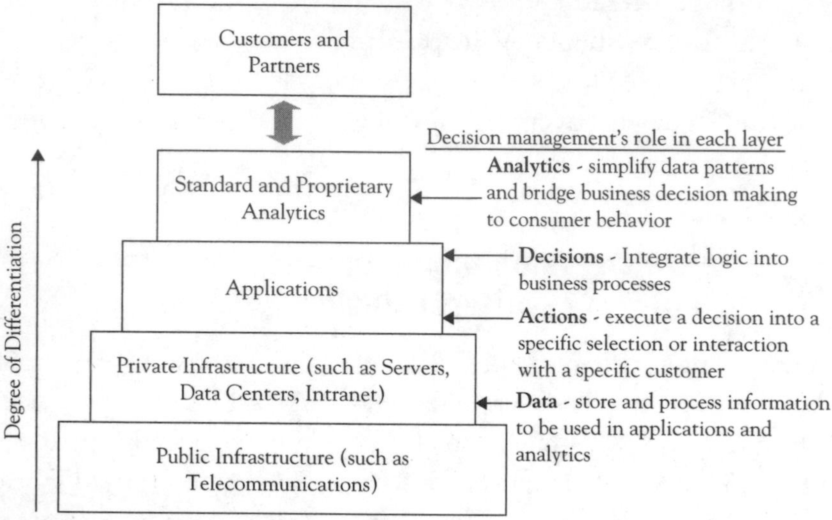

Source: Adapted with permission from C. K. Prahalad and M. S. Krishnan, *The New Age of Innovation: Driving Co-Created Value Through Global Networks* (McGraw-Hill, 2008), 54.

logic and integrate data and analytics into a business process that can improve business performance. Much of this software is also integrated into points of customer interaction—such as call center screens, voice-response units, websites, text messaging, ATMs, and point-of-sale devices.

- *The analytic layer* is wide open. Some businesses will have no capability, others will have pockets of sophistication, and still others will bet their business on analytics. However sophisticated or capable the company, the application layer is where people's foresight, creativity, and discipline can create a competitive asset that is hard to duplicate. Every company—the people and the technology—finds different patterns and makes sense out of oceans of data differently. Analytics is also the element that enables businesses to automate decisions with more confidence that those decisions are accurate, timely, and cost-effective.

How Decision Management Makes Knowledge Technologists More Productive

Many studies of the U.S. economy have demonstrated the positive relationship between IT investment and productivity. For example, since 1995, productivity growth in the United States has averaged more than 2.5 percent per year, compared with the average growth rate of about 1.4 percent per year over the preceding twenty years.[2] Decision management continues to support this trend, especially among knowledge technologists. To illustrate this, let's look at a couple of brief case studies.

Case Study: An Insurance Company Increased Revenue by 35 Percent with the Same Number of Staff

With more automation and more sophisticated decision management systems running inside companies in the future, we expect to see more operational managers making fewer micro decisions related to their particular responsibility. As a result, they will be able to use more of their time and talent to be more creative and to think about how their decisions fit into the larger corporate picture. With more of the day-to-day decisions automated, they can take responsibility for more decisions that contribute to the competitive position of the business.

For example, one of the largest auto insurers in Michigan changed in the last few years from using its centralized group of underwriters who manually reviewed all insurance policy applications to a process where they review only 1 percent of those applications. Once the automated decision management system was installed, underwriters turned their attention from evaluating individual policies to helping agents with their blocks of business. This led to a tripling of independent agents and a 35-percent increase in revenue, with the same number of staff. The automation required analytics and coding of three thousand business rules into a rules management system.

Case Study: Air Products Reduced Product Development Time from Forty-Five Days to One Day

Another Fair Isaac client, Air Products is a U.S.-based producer of specialty gases, performance materials, and equipment and services for industrial and health care markets worldwide. The company embedded the expertise and decisions of hundreds of dispersed product configuration specialists into a decision management system to speed the flow of materials and end products to the customer, systematically capturing decisions that specialists formerly made regarding such things as the sources of gases, recipes for mixing gases, and inspection routines for different mixes. Previously, the process required multiple layers of approval for complex configurations. Also, configuration experts are hard to hire and train because their knowledge is so specialized. Automating the decision process reduced the product creation cycle time *from forty-five days to a single day.*

Although rules-based expert systems first appeared a number of years ago, the newer systems, such as the one deployed by Air Products, has qualities the earlier systems did not. In particular, it is not a stand-alone application, and the new knowledge it captures is used to improve the product creation process.

Societal Trends That Are Changing the Way We Do Business

Automating Air Products' decision process reduced the product creation cycle time from 45 days to a single day.

The digital age is transforming the possibilities of established companies to find meaning in data and of entrepreneurs to create new business models. The next sections of this chapter describe how companies' business models need to change to accommodate the changes we're seeing in society—specifically:

- How an increasingly cashless economy makes it even easier to track customer spending patterns and develop more robust customer profiles
- How companies in different markets who have the same customers are *collaborating*—because they don't compete with each other—to share data about those customers
- How new technologies are being developed to better use *unstructured data*—such as videos of customers—to add to a company's knowledge of its customers' purchasing habits
- How social networking sites (such as Facebook) can provide new ways to target and advertise to people who are willingly providing information on these sites about their interests and preferences
- How companies in emerging markets (such as Latin America, Eastern Europe, India, and China) are starting to compete internationally for their share of consumer spending—which means they're also interested in using analytic tools and decision management techniques so they can better serve those customers and increase their own bottom lines

Credit card and debit card use in the United States quintupled from 10 percent to 52 percent of transactions from 1995 to 2003.

Trend #1: An Increasingly Cashless Economy Enables Tracking of More Customer Data

Obviously, there is a limit to what companies can learn about consumer behavior when people pay with cash. Fortunately, as cashless commerce spreads, there will be much more data on what people are buying, when, where, how often, in what quantities, with what other products, and so much more that marketers will want to know. As far back as the 1950s, when credit cards were invented, futurists have been predicting that physical paper and coins would eventually disappear, but it wasn't really until the Internet went commercial that cashless commerce took off. For example, consider the following stats and trends:

- In the United States, cash payments dropped from 60 percent to 30 percent of all consumer transactions between 1995 and 2003.
- Credit card and debit card use in the United States quintupled from 10 percent to 52 percent of transactions during that same time period, 1995 to 2003.
- In 2006, consumers in the United States used debit cards to make more than 350 billion transactions of less than $5 (which are called *micropayments*), totaling $1.32 trillion.

The tipping point for cashless commerce is predicted to be when small e-payments—that is, those for less than $25— overtake cash.[3]

Trend #2: Multiple Companies Sharing Data About Customers They Have in Common

Merchants, credit card companies, and banks also have incentives to work through ways to encourage e-payments. After all, advanced data mining, combined with algorithms to analyze the data, give all of these companies new ways to compete for consumers' discretionary spending.

Case Study: MasterCard Develops a Commerce Coalition with Some of Its Merchants

In 2007, MasterCard led an experiment in a data sharing collaboration among four MasterCard bank issuers and four merchants: a big-box home improvement retailer, a furniture retailer, a video rental chain, and a restaurant chain. Study of the data showed that people who are do-it-yourselfers, rent movies, and dine out regularly at moderately priced restaurants are quite alike in their tastes and spending habits. This commerce coalition aggregated and analyzed purchase data of customers of each business.

Because the participating merchants served the same customer segment, but were not direct competitors, they could share customer data to increase sales volume and improve target marketing. The coalition pooled data and analyzed spending patterns by account behavior. The card issuers provided account information but no personal information. New forms of e-commerce between these entities have been slow to develop because the different interests of merchants, credit card issuers, and banks are not always in harmony, but this experiment showed they could collaborate.[4]

Case Study: Third-Party Aggregators Collect Data from Various Sources

Third-party data aggregators have been serving companies for many years—for example, credit bureaus are aggregators of data for lenders. In today's cashless commerce environment, different aggregators are emerging to serve consumers. This arrangement is a three-party system among consumers, product and service providers, and data aggregators—with the data aggregators in the middle. Here are just a few examples of companies that are doing this:

- *Mint.com* is a personal financial management online service that aggregates data from its customers' credit-card providers, banks, and credit unions. The site uploads customers' account information and allows advertisers to offer them specialized services. In return, each night Mint.com connects to the credit card and financial services providers in the network to update its customers' daily activity, including their purchases and checking account balances. The service can also categorize personal spending, and it can shop for better rates on savings products and credit cards.[5]

- *Google Health* is a division that Google launched in October 2007: it bills itself as a "safe, secure, and free" service for individuals to keep and update all their health information in one place—including medical records from doctors, hospitals, and pharmacies—and as a place to search for health service providers.[6]

- *HealthVault* is a similar service offered by Microsoft: a platform for helping health care providers and other professionals put all their information online. For example, a hospital could use HealthVault to design a software program that takes data from a blood pressure monitor and shares it electronically with physicians.

> *Google Health offers a "safe, secure, and free" service for individuals to keep and update all their health information in one place—including medical records from doctors, hospitals, and pharmacies.*

It is notable in this case study that both Google and Microsoft are going for personalized and convenient access to health data, and they are also dealing with significant regulatory complexity.

It is also significant that these services—which are handling health and financial data, which in our experience are the most sensitive types of personal data—were launched by well-known and trusted brands. Google was identified as the number one company in 2008, in terms of its company reputation, according to a Harris market research survey.[7] Notably, Google replaced Microsoft, which had topped the list in 2007, and it beat Johnson & Johnson, which had been the top-ranked company from 2006 back to the survey's first year in 1999. Although 70 percent of respondents said the "reputation of corporate America is poor," they also said they would do business with and invest in companies that are known for their good corporate reputations.

Privacy experts generally agree that roughly 50 percent of consumers are willing to have their transactional behavior analyzed at an individual level, provided they understand the scope of such use and the benefits they can expect in return. Therefore, corporate reputations are going to become more important—especially with respect to how a company handles data.

Trend #3: New Technologies Being Developed to Enable the Use of Unstructured Data

Companies are just beginning to tap into *unstructured data* (for example, e-mails, documents, video, and pictures), which represents a new source of raw materials to better inform decisions. Not surprisingly, the real power in unstructured data is realized when it can be quantified and analyzed by analytic and business experts. For instance, to convert video and pictures into useful information, you first need a human expert with insight to define the value in the video or in the picture.

For example, the engineering organization at General Motors has turned digitized videos of customer focus groups into a powerful support tool to make design decisions. A team of twelve GM analysts conducted several focus groups a month, capturing thirty hours of video for each session—which obviously meant that *thousands* of hours of video accumulated quickly. By digitizing the content, technicians were able to spend half as much time searching for focus group findings from the raw video; in addition, product analysts could load the searchable content onto their laptops.

However, costs and the amount of storage space are constraints. Although the cost of data storage is constantly decreasing, the digital data being created each year is already straining storage capacity, and the problem will worsen: "The amount of information created, captured, or replicated exceeded available storage for the first time in 2007 . . . and by 2011, almost half of the digital universe will not have a permanent home."[8]

Also, according to McKinsey, data storage is one of the fastest-growing parts of the IT budget. Enterprise-wide transactional systems, massive data warehouses, and explosive growth in e-mail traffic are sources of data growth. Demand for storage has been rising by more than 50 percent annually, even faster than the unit cost of storage has fallen. If storage costs continue to rise at a rapid pace, it may make it more difficult for companies to store and create business value from unstructured data.[9]

Trend #4: Obtaining Data from Social Networking Sites

The idea of human beings relating to each other in *social networks* has been recognized since the 1800s. In fact, the term was coined in the 1950s and has been studied by sociologists, psychologists, and marketers for decades. Nevertheless, the Internet and other network technologies give the phenomenon a new lease on life—and new ways to study it.

Social networking sites are potentially even more valuable to advertisers because people with common interests not only congregate at these sites but also spend a lot of time defining themselves as individuals.

Joseph Sirosh, who once led Fair Isaac's Advanced Technology Solutions group, often said, "You are known by the company you keep." Internet advertising strategies use that same principle to target websites that attract people with specific interests. Social networking sites are potentially even more valuable to advertisers because people with common interests not only congregate at these sites but also spend a lot of time defining themselves as individuals.

Still, many digital prospectors have overpaid for their purchases of social networking sites. Now they are struggling to figure out how to make money from advertising models. We need to distinguish the struggle of the moment for advertisers and marketers and the *future value* of the data generated by social networks. The real question is, how deep can analytics go to extract consumer insights and predictions on social networks, and how will it affect the operating decisions of companies? Perhaps it will be Coca-Cola, Pepsi, and P&G that prove to be the innovators. More likely, though, clever entrepreneurs will be first to figure out better business models than the current crop, and large companies will be watching.

Yochai Benkler is the Berkman Professor of Entrepreneurial Legal Studies at Harvard and faculty codirector of the Berkman Center for Internet and Society. Benkler postulates that as digital sharing grows, consumer-to-consumer communication (that is, word of mouth) will become more valuable to marketers. Benkler specializes in the study of open-source management, and he envisions a day when consumers shopping in retail stores can use their mobile phones to scan a radio-frequency identification tag (RFID) tag on a product they are interested in purchasing and instantly access peer-to-peer consumer rating sites such as Epinions. In this market conversation, Benkler said that corporate marketers will become "more intermediaries to the community of users, to engage the users more in the design process and the distribution process, treating their users as co-producers of value." The example he uses is a website devoted to kite surfing, with aerospace engineers (an affinity group that tends to be passionate about kite surfing) congregating on the site to design solutions that are immediately taken up by manufacturers.[10]

How might co-creation and open-source management evolve? One concept might be if innovative companies had a special arrangement to share their data with a peer-to-peer production community, such as the kite surfing group, thereby reaping the rewards

> *What if consumers could pick and choose what businesses to invite into their social networks, or their private profiles, and shut out companies they did not like?*

of exclusive data sharing and participation in this capable customer group's innovation process.

Or think about this: on Facebook, you invite people to view your profile. What if consumers could pick and choose what businesses to invite into their social networks, or their private profiles, and shut out companies they did not like? The Harris Interactive survey suggests that consumers are watching corporate behavior, and it is as important to consumers as it is to corporations that are watching themselves. It will be interesting to see how this plays out in the real world and in virtual commerce.

Virtual worlds may seem strange to some people, but they are growing in popularity. These sites are laboratories for new insights into human behavior—and they are not insignificant moneymakers. For example, consider the following examples:

- In January 2007, participants in Second Life (probably the best-known virtual world) spent nearly $5 million (that's virtual dollars) on about 4.2 million (virtual) transactions involving buying or selling (virtual) clothes or buildings.

- As of August 2007, Second Life had approximately 9 million members, up from 3.5 million in January.

- Movie Tickets.com is building a virtual island in Second Life, complete with a theater that shows trailers of "first life" (that is, real-world) movies and lists show times for real-life local theaters.

- Netherlands-based ING, in partnership with Rivers Run Red (a 3-D interactive content developer), is building a virtual Holland within Second Life, where residents can own (virtual) land and run (virtual) businesses.

- In August 2007, Disney purchased the children's virtual-world Club Penguin for $350 million in cash, plus up to $350 million more, depending on the website's profits in 2008 and 2009. Club Penguin, launched in October 2005, was designed as a virtual world for children to play games or just hang out with virtual friends.[11]

Marketers will want to learn more about what people are "consuming" in these virtual worlds—and to find out whether that information carries over into the real world.

Clearly, as more people become interested in virtual worlds, marketers will follow that trail: they'll naturally want to learn more about what people are "consuming" in these virtual worlds—and to find out whether that information carries over into the real world.

Trend #5: Companies from Emerging Markets Competing for Their Share of Consumer Spending

In 2008, IBM surveyed and interviewed 1,130 CEOs from forty countries and thirty-two industries, seeking their views on what they consider the most significant strategic challenges and opportunities for global corporations, including the new competitors from emerging markets. Companies represented included firms from developed economies, with more than $500 million in revenues and up, and firms from emerging economies, with revenues of more than $250 million.[12] The study painted a picture of the new global enterprises, mainly from Latin America, India, China, and Eastern Europe. Here are just a few of the emerging multinationals that just a few years ago were unknown outside their home countries:

- India's Tata Group—founded in 1968 as a private trading firm ("Tata" was the founder's surname), it is now a huge conglomerate comprising ninety-six companies in seven business sectors on six continents, with 350,000 global employees. However, it's likely that few people in the United States had ever heard of the company until 2008, when it acquired the Jaguar and Land Rover brands from the Ford Motor Company.
- India's ICICI—India's largest private sector bank (in terms of market capitalization) and second largest bank (in assets, with a total of the equivalent of $100 billion as of March 2008), it is a growing international competitor, with offices in eighteen countries. We offer a case study about this intriguing company later in this chapter.

- China's Haier—the world's fourth largest manufacturer of white goods (that is, appliances, including refrigerators and other kitchen appliances, air conditioners, washing machines, TVs, even personal computers and mobile phones), it has 240 subsidiary companies and more than 50,000 employees around the world.

- Mexico's Cemex—founded in 1906 as a small local business, this building materials company has grown to become one of the world's leaders in cement production and more, with operations in fifty countries and sixty thousand employees worldwide.

Domestically and internationally, many of these companies are competing aggressively for their share of the new consumer's spending. McKinsey estimates that almost a billion new consumers will enter the global marketplace by 2015, as household incomes rise above the level of $5,000 in annual household income in all developing countries, which McKinsey says is when people generally begin to spend on discretionary goods.[13]

From now to 2015, consumer spending power in emerging economies will increase from $4 trillion to more than $9 trillion–nearly the current spending power of Western Europe.

"I watched the banking industry in Turkey do in four years what it took twenty years to do in the U.K. These countries are going to leapfrog developed markets."

–Robert Duque-Ruberio, Fair Isaac vice-president

Demand for consumer products and services is rising faster in emerging economies than anywhere else in the world. From now to 2015, consumer spending power in emerging economies will increase from $4 trillion to more than $9 trillion—nearly the current spending power of Western Europe. Or as one real estate CEO from India commented in the IBM report, "In India, four hundred million consumers will demand new housing in the next twenty years—that's more real estate than the United States has built since the Second World War."

In 1990, only nineteen companies from developing countries were in the Global Fortune 500; in 2007, that number had risen to seventy-four.[14] The new generation of multinationals will also be leaders in the use of analytics and decision management. For details, let's look at two case studies.

Case Study: Turkey's Largest Retail Bank Competes via Cell Phones

Akbank T.A.S. is the largest of four retail banks in Turkey vying for consumer lending and credit card services aimed at middle-income customers, many of whom are using banking services for the first time. Turkey has a total population of approximately 72 million, and as is typical of emerging economies, there is a large income disparity between the ultra-affluent and the rest of the population. Retail banks such as Akbank have historically served a small, high-net-worth customer base, but in Turkey these days, growth depends on winning over the middle-income consumer and consumers who are using banking services for the first time.

Akbank has been able to build several layers of IT infra-structure from scratch. Because of this, it isn't burdened with the product-centric legacy of IT systems of banks in the United States and Western Europe. Robert Duque-Ruberio, a Fair Isaac vice-president based in London who has worked with Akbank since 2000, confirms this: "I watched the banking industry in Turkey do in four years what it took twenty years to do in the U.K. These countries are going to leapfrog developed markets. What's exciting is that they see new things and are willing to try them."

Akbank operates Turkey's second largest consumer banking branch network. In the summer of 2003, Akbank managers approached Fair Isaac with an idea of creating an online channel to lower the bank's cost of acquiring new customers and to increase convenience for its customers. Cell phone usage in Turkey has been rising steadily for years, and home-based internet access is now more common. Akbank's managers decided that making a cell phone a channel to apply for a loan would stimulate even higher volumes of applications than the Internet. Applications are carefully screened using credit risk scores. The strategy was to use technology to offer consumers speed and convenience while simultaneously managing customer profitability and losses among segments with different risk profiles.

In December 2005, the mobile phone-based loan origination program, called CepKredi (which in Turkish means "speedy cell credit"), was launched. A customer can be anywhere when he or she decides to dial in for a loan—at home watching television, walking down the street, or riding a train. The CepKredi phone number, 44400011, is heavily advertised on television, in print media, and on billboards.

When the consumer calls to apply for a credit card or a loan, an interactive voice response system asks eleven questions. Completing the application takes less than five minutes, an instant credit scoring analysis is done, and within twenty minutes the consumer receives a voicemail or an SMS text message on their cell phone stating whether the application has been accepted or rejected.

The result? In 2006, approximately fifty-three thousand people received loans through Akbank's mobile phone credit service. Moreover, here's even more impressive growth:

- Since 2005, Akbank's retail customer base has grown to more than 5.4 million retail customers.
- In 2007, the annual report noted that 2.35 million customers per month now use Akbank's mobile channel, and 61 percent of the bank's transactions are carried out through these channels.
- Akbank has seven hundred thousand internet branch customers.

- Customers carry out 32 percent of the bank's transactions on the Internet.
- Akbank has about 1,615 ATMs—10 percent of all ATMs in the country.
- Approximately 1.9 million people a month use Akbank ATMs.

Akbank is demonstrating the leap-frog advantage of established emerging market retail banks. By investing early and strategically, Akbank now has a head start over local and international competitors. And by integrating decision management technology into its IT infrastructure, it has the databases to capture all the internal and external data on a given customer. (In Turkey, the government-supported credit bureau was established in 2002.) Akbank's credit management system, which includes behavior scoring and adaptive control technology, covers the entire credit life cycle, including prospecting for customers, underwriting loans, and managing customer accounts. The system runs through 17 different paths, 620 rules, 390 strategies, 330 scenarios, and 5,327 steps.

Decision management is also critical to Akbank's strategy of aggressive but controlled market share growth, as it expands into new middle-income and "unbanked" segments. Akbank will need to be agile and vigilant in controlling delinquency and fraud. Akbank's creative use of electronic channels has put it in a strong position to realize these additional goals:

- To take advantage of data on prospective customers and current customers for cross-selling products
- To increase the efficiency and effectiveness of marketing initiatives
- To increase profit per customer

In 2006, CitiGroup bought a 20 percent stake in Akbank for $3.1 billion. CitiGroup's global brand and technology is now combined powerfully with Akbank's knowledge of the market. The collaboration is specifically about growing the retail bank, joint investments in technology, and managerial sharing. Finally, although Akbank currently serves only the Turkish market, expansion into Europe is on its radar.

Case Study: India's Second Largest Bank Competes for Rural, Urban, and Global Business

In India, ICICI is another established domestic banking brand that has transformed itself in a few short years, and with both domestic and global ambitions. ICICI was not a consumer bank when it was founded in 1955. Formerly known as the Industrial Credit and Investment Corporation of India, ICICI was a state-owned enterprise that provided project financing to Indian corporations. A product of India's liberalization policies in the 1990s, today, ICICI has come a long way:

- ICICI is India's largest private sector bank in market capitalization.
- It is India's second largest bank in terms of assets.
- It is a growing international competitor, with a presence in eighteen countries.
- In 2000, ICICI's consumer banking business had fewer than a million customers; by June 2006, that number had risen almost tenfold, to 9.5 million.
- Its asset base grew from around $250 million in 1996 to $80 billion in 2006 and to almost $100 billion by the end of March 2008.
- As of 2007, ICICI had about a 30-percent market share overall in retail financing products, including credit cards, mortgage lending, and personal lending.

Analytic technology was not relevant for the old ICICI, but it is now central to the bank's growth and success. In the next decade, retail banking is expected to be one of India's fastest-growing markets. Nearly 70 percent of the population is under thirty-five years of age, according to the 2003 government census, and banking services are a new phenomenon for most of the population. ICICI is aiming to be the leader in the domestic urban and rural markets (where 70 percent of the population lives) and to be the bank of choice for Indians living abroad in North America and Europe.

Like Akbank in Turkey, ICICI is using analytics and information technology to accelerate new customer growth and manage its risk exposure. It has positioned itself as a high-tech innovator, offering cost-effective and convenient banking through online banking, ATMs, and mobile phone banking. ICICI was the first bank in India to offer internet banking. In 2008, ICICI introduced iMobile banking: customers connect to the Internet using their mobile phones to do transactions with the bank. With the growth in e-channels, branches are now more valuable to ICICI as points of sale for products.

When ICICI created its first in-house analytic team in 2001, there were only twenty-five analysts whose sole responsibility was to track market conditions and delinquencies. India did not have a credit bureau until 2005, so when ICICI began developing its first predictive models, it had no external source of data on consumer credit behavior. Moreover, because ICICI was new to the consumer banking market, it also didn't have internal data. Therefore the first in-house scorecards were constructed without data.

Now ICICI has large internal databases and has refined its scorecards, which are used in credit card services, mortgage, auto, and two-wheeler (bicycle) lending. Better customer segmentations increase the bank's precision and agility in monitoring delinquencies and adjusting credit lines. Segmentations are also used for transaction-based target marketing programs and to forecast accurate foreclosure rates.

Analytics has also been a powerful tool for ICICI to expand preapproved credit line offers. An ATM-based overdraft service for checking accounts is one of the bank's most novel services. ICICI has also developed scores to monitor the risk behaviors of a single customer across multiple products.

ICICI and other Indian banks have an edge over the foreign global banks competing for their slice of the new urban consumer class. The domestic bank's advantage is even more pronounced in rural areas. Using technology and imagination, ICICI is coming up with radically different retail services for a radically different client. For example, rural bank lending might include loans for growing crops or buying a buffalo, as well for education, health care, and mortgages. Because there is no data, ICICI has been creative in characterizing rural segments: for example, an "affluent farmer" is someone who purchases high-tech equipment and has a large land holding, whereas a "normal farmer" owns small plots of land and is often employed by affluent farmers. ICICI is developing its microfinance lending for as little as $100, and terms of payment are also personalized—for example, for a farmer, it might be adjusted to the milk yield of a single buffalo.

ICICI is testing technologies to promote connectivity in areas where there is no electricity, much less wireless. In partnership with other Indian banks and with IBM, ICICI has started a separate company to focus on technology solutions for the rural sector. One initiative is to create a biometric card for rural customers to be used for every transaction, to protect identity and facilitate service delivery to areas where several villages might share a single banking kiosk.

How Decision Management Is Changing in Different Industries

In addition to the major changes in how data is being used and analyzed because of the five sweeping trends just described, decision management is also changing in different industries. To better understand these changes, in 2004 Fair Isaac partnered with the Opinion Research Corporation to survey top managers working in a variety of industries:

ICICI was the first bank in India to offer internet banking. And in 2008, ICICI introduced iMobile banking: customers connect to the Internet using their mobile phones to do transactions with the bank.

- Retail banking
- Credit cards
- Health care
- Insurance
- Telecom

We surveyed two hundred senior IT professionals (VPs, CIOs, and CTOs) from Fortune 1,000 companies in these industries to learn how their companies had adopted decision management technology. Here are just some of the more interesting results:

- Almost all respondents (93 percent) said that frontline operational decisions impacted their company's profitability, with 61 percent rating this impact as significant.
- But only a fraction of decisions have been automated: more than half of the respondents (53 percent) said their companies had automated less than 25 percent of these decisions.
- A significant minority (42 percent) was aware of the potential for predictive analytics to deliver a return on their data investment, but only 12 percent were currently using them.

> Ninety-three percent of senior managers surveyed said frontline operational decisions impacted their company's profitability . . . But 53 percent also said their companies had automated less than 25 percent of these decisions.

Naturally, different industries will adopt decision management technologies at different paces. The next (and final) sections of this chapter look at some key industries that are leaders in decision management: financial services, health care, and of course, retail.

How Decision Management Is Improving in the Financial Services Industry

Banks have fifty years of experience in gaining high returns from decision management investments, and insurance companies are closing in on a similar level of sophistication and yield. Connecting decisions for managing customer relationships and multiple products, coupled with advances in transaction analytics and optimization technology, will yield another level of profitability increases for financial services companies.

As consolidation among consumer banks around the world continues, and new competitors from emerging market countries go global, retail banks are under more pressure than ever before to become customer-centric. Changing consumer expectations are also forcing this change. Customers are looking for new ways to interact with companies and form relationships, whether it happens through relationships with such banks as ING Direct and Prosper.com or from experiences outside of banking with such companies as Netflix and Apple.

Today, few financial services companies have the right capabilities to capitalize on the convergence of customer-centricity and decision management. In 2008, Fair Isaac partnered with Tower Group to conduct a survey of senior risk managers and credit executives at the top fifty U.S. banks and credit card issuers. We asked them their views on connected decision making: more than 80 percent said it is "critical" or "important" to make connected decisions across product lines and throughout the credit product lifecycle (prospect marketing, origination, customer management, collections). Despite this interest, *fewer than 5 percent* currently have a single, unified decision management system in place to do so.

Another way to connect decisions is to use decision optimization technology to look at conflicting objectives and trade-offs that may span different areas of a bank. The survey showed that only 30 percent were deploying any optimization techniques at all, although again, 80 percent are interested in doing so. Large financial services institutions tended to see the establishment of an enterprise decision management system as a slow, complex process, but they are becoming more convinced of its necessity.

By 2015, 80 percent of European banks will replace traditional *age-based* segmentation models with *behavior-based* programs. The Tower Group's analyst Ralph Silva said these investments will initially enable a bank to improve its marketing by identifying customers who favor other brands but who still have accounts with them. Banks that use behavior-based segmentation of customers will be better able to identify unprofitable and high-risk individuals who should be moved to lower-cost, technology-oriented channels. Focus groups and standardized segments will give way to bank-targeted segments determined by customers' transaction activity, based on their debit and credit card payment usage, as provided to banks by card issuers.[15]

Peer-to-peer lenders such as Prosper.com and competitors Zopa, Lending Club, and Virgin Money USA will not put the traditional commercial banks in developed economies out of business, but they are a creative market force that puts positive pressure on financial services providers to improve their performance and value propositions. Today, the leading P2P lenders are operating in the United States and the U.K. but they will spread to other countries.

Furthermore, P2P lending has greater potential and relevance in developing countries where formalized banking is not as well established among certain populations. P2P lending is already proving to be a powerful way to bring first-time users of formal banking into the system.

How Decision Management Is Improving in the Health Care Industry

Health care is just entering the digital age, as information is becoming more standardized and is captured in computer systems. The health care future, for reasons of both cost and quality of life, will focus on prevention, prediction, early detection, and early treatment of diseases. This is where analytics can be especially useful. Given the significant privacy concerns, consumers will have to see significant benefits to sharing their information. One appeal of information technology will be encouraging better health habits; for instance, by reminding people with chronic diseases when they need to renew their prescriptions or schedule a check-up appointment.

Expanding networks of accessible medical data is important, but there are many questions to be answered—such as these:

- Can we improve matching of symptoms to diseases?
- Will more data make evidence-based medicine in treatment selection more common? The Center for Evidence-Based Medicine defines this practice as "the conscientious, explicit, and judicious use of current best evidence in making decisions about the care of individual patients."
- How can we use data to reduce medical errors? For example, in the United States—a country that spends more per capita on health care than any other—as many as ninety-eight thousand Americans die each year *from preventable medical errors* during hospitalization.[16] Moreover, 35 percent of physicians and 42 percent of the public said they had *personally experienced errors* in their own or a family member's care.[17] Finally, the economic costs associated with these errors—in terms of lost income, disability, and health care expenses—are as high as $29 billion annually,[18] and preventable

medication errors alone are estimated to increase hospital costs by about $2 billion nationwide.

Rules engines and analytics can be instrumental in tackling all these challenges. Think about a single process: individual pharmacists who keep track of a patient's drug reaction history. If patient data and problematic interactions were available in a common database, the two could be matched to provide more timely warnings or actions.

Progress on electronic medical records has been held back by loose and overlapping technical standards and poor interoperability among different types of health care information systems sold by hundreds of different vendors.

In the United States, patients and providers are warming to electronic health records. Users are more comfortable with keeping online records, and health-care organizations themselves are more motivated to keep information digitally, thanks to government incentives and a desire to please web-savvy patients. Progress on electronic medical records has been held back by loose and overlapping technical standards and poor interoperability among different types of health care information systems sold by hundreds of different vendors. Another obstacle may be a payment system that offers little financial incentive for most health care providers to invest in using e-medical records internally, let alone sharing them externally.

Decision management and analytics can be a key driver of adoption of electronic medical records. There is a parallel to banking: banks originally contributed data to the credit bureaus so that they could make better decisions in return (for example, so they could understand customers better when deciding whether to originate loans). If they did not have that common decision goal, the credit bureaus would never have been created. Articulating these common goals and demonstrating improved decision making as a key benefit are both critical to unleashing this potential in health care.

How Decision Management Is Improving in Retail Businesses

In the consumer products value chain, historically, the product manufacturers have not had a direct connection to the end consumer, and retailers have been guarded about sharing sales information and other data. Increasingly, however, consumer packaged goods (CPG) leaders, such as Coca-Cola and Procter & Gamble, have been working more closely with their retail distributors. Consultants at Booz & Co. call this relationship *shelf-centered collaboration*. For instance, P&G's distribution channel partners supply point-of-sale data to P&G's consumer-driven supply chain system, which uses automated analytics to make product manufacturing and distribution decisions. For example, P&G monitors the impact of specific promotional campaigns on store sales. It is also using the system to significantly improve inventory management, particularly out-of-stock performance. For consumers (specifically, the person who does the laundry), out-of-stock performance means there is no Tide on the supermarket shelf for two weeks in a row.[19] Although this is an unlikely scenario, it is a simple example of how the divide between how companies think and how *consumers* think is narrowing.

Investments by CPG manufacturers and their distributors are changing this dynamic by using data, analytics, and interactive media to forge relationships with consumers. CPG companies and retailers have had a partnership of information starting back in the 1980s with category management. The style of partnerships and strength of influences on the consumer are changing dramatically.

Putting aside the potential of virtual worlds (described earlier in the chapter), in the real world, personalization of customer experiences is an important trend. Imagine being in a traditional retail setting and feeling as though the entire store and the store experience had been built around *you*. This was the magic of the classic family American department stores in their heyday. Technology will make this a reality for stores of all scale in the next five years. For those retailers adopting this style of retailing, they will be able to cost-effectively offer a differentiated experience to their customers.

How can this be done? There are changes occurring at several levels:

- *Data*—access to rich transaction data, especially loyalty data; in other words, which products were bought at which locations, at what time, in which combination, and by which customer?
- *Analytics*—optimization to fine-tune the customer experience; analytics using unstructured data to achieve a more free-flowing conversation with customers.
- *Decisions*—balancing customer preferences against company profitability to select the right actions.
- *Action*—more real-time presentations of actions; more continuity of actions across channels; more dialogue and customer-driven actions.

For example, the Macy's department store chain in the United States says information technology "is playing a larger and increasingly crucial role as we increase convenience for customers, speed of transactions, improve merchandising and operate more efficiently."[20] This could be a turning point for the venerable retailer, which has struggled to make its strategy to become a national retailer pay off. From 2005 to 2007, Macy's Inc. (previously Federated Department Stores) went on an acquisition spree that has made it the largest department store retail operating company in the United States. In February 2005, Federated acquired May Department Stores for $11 billion in stock, creating the nation's second largest department store chain, with $30 billion in annual sales and more than a thousand stores. Since then, Macy's has acquired all the old-time family department stores in major cities—including the landmark Marshall Field's store on Chicago's North State Street, Dayton Hudson's flagship store on Nicollette Mall (just around the corner from Fair Isaac's headquarters in Minneapolis), and the Strawbridge & Clothier flagship store in Philadelphia. Macy's also acquired many smaller chains from coast to coast in the United States; for example, Bullocks in the South, Kauffman's in the Midwest, and multiple store brands acquired with its purchase of May Department Stores.

The depth of locals' loyalty to their home-town stores surprised Macy's executives. Initially, the strategy was to win over the loyalists, but that proved difficult. In Chicago, when Macy's moved into the State Street store in 2005, customers took to the streets in protest. Hundreds of angry Chicago natives and long-time Marshall Field's customers gathered under the famous Marshall Field's clock on the day the Macy's sign went up on State Street. For weeks, protesters continued to gather on State Street to solicit support to take back their store.[21]

Meanwhile, these customers started shopping elsewhere. After two years of declining sales in the flagship store, Macy's changed its strategy. Rather than try to mollify the old-timers, it decided to attract new customers with the new, modern Macy's experience. In February 2006, Macy's appointed a new chief marketing officer to oversee the nationwide rebranding of all its acquired stores and chains to the Macy's brand. Using a variety of analytic techniques and technology, Macy's is betting that it can get the national momentum in revenues and sales it needs to succeed as a company by infusing insights about customers in critical merchandising, marketing, and other operational decisions, store by store and customer by customer.

Retailers including Best Buy and Tesco have demonstrated that store layout can be tailored to specific customer segments' needs by looking at transaction data and then optimizing product mix by locality.

Having spent billions of dollars to create this company, Macy's has a big challenge—and one could argue that without the analytics, it cannot succeed.

A second way retailers can use advanced decision management is to make personalized decisions in real time for individual consumers. This new customer experience will use transaction data and analytics to look at the logical sequence of customer actions, and it could be up to seven times more accurate than the basic analytic state-of-the-market today. We call this capability *best next action* because it predicts which offer will mostly likely lead a specific, individual customer to come back for a repeat store visit, and which offer will likely increase the size of their market basket on that visit.

Behavioral segmentation is less personal, but it can be just as rewarding for the company and consumer. For example, retailers including Best Buy and Tesco have demonstrated that store layout can be increasingly tailored to specific customer segments' needs by looking at transaction data and then optimizing product mix by locality. Retailers will move from having the right mix to also having the right products placed in the right areas, so that the consumer can easily navigate through the store to pick up related items. These store traffic analysis and placement decisions will be supported by optimization techniques that balance many complex decision trade-offs.

For example, the decision to have many product placements and "facings" (that is, when the label faces the customer) to serve a wide customer base must be balanced against the desire to have a small number of product facings that are relevant and easy to find. There are also trade-offs between margin and shopping cart revenue. Low-margin products may be a bridge from one product category to another to expand the overall size of the shopping cart. Today's optimization technology can address the complexities involved in optimizing billions of potential combinations (thousands of product SKUs, thousands of potential placement locations, and millions of consumers). Placement will also be improved by analytics using unstructured data, such as video footage of customers walking through the store.

With digital distribution and interactive communication, will consumer packaged goods companies and dot-com intermediaries forge such a strong relationship with consumers that physical stores will become obsolete? At this point, it is hard to say, but decision management will play a key role in choosing the winners and losers of this power shift in all worlds and venues.

Concluding Thoughts

How is this book going to make you think differently about operational decision making? In one sense, it is critical to survival; or, as Jack Welch once put it, "If the rate of change inside an organization is less than the rate of change outside . . . the end is in sight." Your decisions are a core means to respond to outside changes—particularly changes in consumer behavior.

This is why decision management provides the critical link between strategy and execution. Given the importance and the size of that gap in most companies, it is an exciting time to be pushing the edge of the envelope with respect to all four decision management components—data, analytics, decisions, and actions.

In addition to surviving, your business will be able to thrive if you achieve the right balance in using decision management to create value for both your customers and your company. Decision management profitably improves the customer experience, turning "or" trade-offs into "and" trade-offs—for example, being able to deliver higher service *and* cut costs. The other beauty of this approach is that your company will be able to see the outcomes and quantify them, pinpointing which individual decisions lead to which financial results. Taking this guesswork out of the equation will open up new possibilities for shaping your customers' experience.

At a pragmatic level, there is money to be made in automating, improving, and connecting decisions. A relentless focus on identifying key decisions and improving them will lead to greater returns than comparable process reengineering or other IT investments have delivered in the past. Still, those investments in process did lay the technical groundwork for improving the decision flow. Those automated processes provide a basis to infuse decisions, connecting company and customer value propositions that generate higher loyalty and revenues at lower costs and risks.

This book attempts to capture the state-of-the-art approaches that businesses are taking today and are likely to take in the next few years. There are endless possibilities in terms of the impact that decision management will have on competitive differentiation in the decades to come. Therefore, you should think of decision management as more of a *journey* than a destination.

To get the value out of the journey, your company needs to invest in it and develop your capabilities. If your company does not have a competency at managing decisions, there is a very disciplined way to get good at it. If your company is sophisticated, there are always new things to apply, given the increasing availability of data and advances in analytics and software. No matter where your company stands, by practicing the disciplines we've described in this book, there are always opportunities to get better and to yield worthwhile business improvements. It is an iterative and progressive approach that amounts to a long and fruitful journey.

In the 1980s, companies invested billions to put a PC on every desk. The 2010s will one day be known as the decade of investing billions to put *intelligence into every decision and every transaction*. Decision management will be the deciding factor in closing the gap between the way your company thinks and the way your customers think. It will be the deciding factor in closing the gap between strategy and execution. Perhaps most important, it will be the deciding factor in determining which companies adapt to changes in consumer behavior so that they survive and thrive into the future. We hope yours is one that does!

Notes

Introduction

1. According to International Data Corporation, an IT market research firm.
2. Ian Davis and Elizabeth Stephens, "Ten Trends to Watch in 2006," *The McKinsey Quarterly* (January 2006).
3. Simon Kennedy and David Matheson, "Data to Die For," *Perspectives* (a Boston Consulting Group publication, Fall 2007).
4. C. K. Prahalad and M. S. Krishnan, *The New Age of Innovation: Driving Co-created Value Through Global Networks* (New York: McGraw-Hill, 2008).
5. "Business by the Numbers," *The Economist*, September 14, 2007.
6. Steve Baker, "Math Will Rock Your World," *BusinessWeek*, January 23, 2006.
7. Steve Lohr, "Reaping Results: Data-Mining Goes Mainstream," *New York Times*, May 20, 2007.
8. Michael Schrage, "Algorithms in the Attic," *Harvard Business Review*, February 2007.

Chapter One

1. Randal Stross, "The Human Touch That May Loosen Google's Grip," *New York Times*, June 24, 2007.
2. Ian Davis and Elizabeth Stephenson, "Ten Trends to Watch in 2006," *The McKinsey Quarterly*, January 2006.

3. "Carte Blank," *Time*, April 28, 1961.
4. Gretchen Morgenson, "Given a Shovel, Americans Dig Deeper Into Debt," *New York Times*, July 20, 2008.
5. Charles Fishman, "Capital One's Marketing Revolution," *Fast Company*, April 1999.
6. Ibid.
7. Clayton M. Christensen and Michael E. Raynor, *The Innovator's Solution: Creating and Sustaining Successful Growth* (Cambridge, MA: Harvard Business School Press, 2003), 221.
8. Roy Williams, "Powers of Ten," Center for Advanced Computing Research, California Institute of Technology, 2000, http://www2.sims.berkeley.edu/research/projects/how-much-info/datapowers.htmlhttp://www.cacr.caltech.edu/~roy/
9. Chris Anderson, "Freenomics," in "The World in 2008," annual outlook issue of *The Economist* (December 2007), 122.
10. "Innovative Management—A Conversation with Lowell Bryan and Gary Hamel," *The McKinsey Quarterly*, October 2007.

Chapter Two

1. Thomas H. Davenport and Jeanne G. Harris, *Competing on Analytics: The New Science of Winning* (Cambridge, MA: Harvard Business School Press, 2007), 6.
2. Clive Humby, Terry Hunt, and Tim Phillips, *Scoring Points: How Tesco Continues to Win Customer Loyalty*, 2nd ed. (Kogan Page, 2007), 231.
3. Ibid., 271
4. "Business by the Numbers," *The Economist*, September 14, 2007.
5. Ibid.
6. Matthew Boyle, "Best Buy's Giant Gamble," *Fortune*, May 29, 2006.

7. Bob Thompson, "Tesco Shines at Loyalty: An Interview with Clive Humby," *CustomerThink*, April 1, 2004.

8. Gary Loveman, "Diamonds in the Data Mine," *Harvard Business Review*, May 2003.

9. Ibid.

10. David Frankland with Christine Spivey Overby and Jennifer Joseph, "Case Study: Harrah's Entertainment Nurtures a Customer Insight Culture," Forrester Research, July 2007.

Chapter Three

1. Christopher Vollmer with Geoffrey Precourt, *Always On: Advertising, Marketing, and Media in an Era of Consumer Control* (New York: McGraw-Hill, 2008), 8.

2. Ibid.

3. Duane D. Santord, "Tapping into Consumers," *Atlanta Journal-Constitution*, Sunday, May 27, 2007.

4. Kate Hughes, "Surveillance Fears Force Norwich to Scrap 'Pay As You Drive' Car Policies," *The Independent*, June 17, 2008.

5. Om Malik, "Is Facebook Beacon a Privacy Nightmare?" GigaOM, November 6, 2007, http://gigaom.com/2007/11/06/facebook-beacon-privacy-issues/.

6. Emily Steel, "Popularity Due to New Efficiencies," *The Wall Street Journal*, June 19, 2007.

7. Ibid.

Chapter Four

1. Davenport and Harris, "Competing on Analytics" (see Chapter Two, note 1).

2. Fishman, "Capital One's Marketing Revolution" (see Chapter One, note 5).

3. Humby, *Scoring Points* (see Chapter Two, note 2).

4. Timothy Hoying, Ashish Jain, and Madhu Mukerji-Miller, "A Better Customer Service Connection," *strategy+business*, Issue 51 (Summer 2008).

Chapter Five

1. Peter Drucker, "The Next Society," *The Economist* survey, November 2001.
2. Ibid.
3. Vollmer with Precourt, *Always On*, 21 (see Chapter Three, note 1).
4. Michael V. Copeland, "The New Careers," *Business 2.0*, May 2007.
5. Ibid.
6. Ibid.
7. Steve Lohr, "Reaping Results: Data-Mining Goes Mainstream," *New York Times*, May 20, 2007.
8. "Best Practices in Marketing Mix Modeling," Forrester Research, August 25, 2005.
9. Frankland with Overby and Joseph, "Case Study: Harrah's Entertainment Nurtures a Customer Insight Culture" (see Chapter Two, note 10).

Chapter Six

1. Steven D. Levitt and Stephen J. Dubner, *Freakonomics: A Rogue Economist Explores the Hidden Side of Everything* (New York: Morrow, 2005), 12.
2. Saul Hansel, "Google Answer to Filing Jobs Is an Algorithm," *New York Times*, January 3, 2007.
3. Dr. John Sullivan, "Google Continues to Innovate in Recruiting and Candidate Assessment," Ere.net, January 8, 2007.
4. Andrew McAfee and Erik Brynjolfsson, "Investing in IT Makes a Competitive Difference," *Harvard Business Review*, July-August 2008.

5. Jack Welch with John Byrne, *Jack: Straight from the Gut* (New York: Business Plus, 2001), 236.

Chapter Seven

1. Charles Lucier and Jan Dyer, "The Crucial Link to Execution," *strategy+business*, Winter 2004.
2. The Economic Report of the President, 2007, by the Chairman of the Council of Economic Advisors.
3. Ted Iacobuzio, analyst with The Tower Group, speaking at the third annual Small Payments Conference in December 2006.
4. "Merchants Team Up to Boost Customer Loyalty and Sales," *MasterCard Advisor*, Issue 2 (2007).
5. Denise Caruso, "Securing Very Important Data: Your Own," *New York Times*, October 7, 2007.
6. Catherine Holahan, "Google's Rx for Health Data," *BusinessWeek*, February 29, 2008.
7. The 9th Annual RQ Reputations of the 60 Most Visible Companies: A Survey of the U.S. General Public, Using the Harris Interactive Quotient, 2008.
8. International Data Corporation, 2007.
9. James M. Kaplan, Rishi Roy, and Rajesh Srinivasaraghavan, "Meeting the Demand for Data Storage," *The McKinsey Quarterly*, June 2008.
10. Bob Garfield, "Inside the New World of Listenomics: How the Open Source Revolution Impacts Your Brands," *Advertising Age*, October 11, 2005.
11. David Furlonger, "The Future of Money," Gartner Financial Services, December 18, 2007.
12. IBM Global CEO Study: Enterprise of the Future, May 5, 2008.
13. Ian Davis and Elizabeth Stephens, "Ten Trends to Watch in 2006," *The McKinsey Quarterly*, January 2006.
14. Gerald Adolph and Justin Pettit, *Merge Ahead: Mastering the Five Enduring Trends of Artful M&A* (New York: McGraw-Hill, 2008).

15. Ralph Silva, "Developing European Banks' Behavior-Based Segmentation Model," Tower Group, July 2007.
16. According to a 1999 report by the Institute of Medicine.
17. According to a 2002 study by the Harvard School of Public Health and the Kaiser Family Foundation.
18. According to the National Academy of Sciences Institute of Medicine.
19. Rich Kauffeld, Johan Sauer, and Sara Bergson, "Partners at the Point of Sale," *strategy+business*, 48 (Autumn 2007).
20. "Macy's Launches New Initiatives to Drive Sales, Earnings," corporate press release, February 6, 2008.
21. Sandra Jones, "Hard-Core Fans Stay Loyal to Brand," *Chicago Tribune*, September 5, 2006.

Appendix A

FAIR ISAAC'S DECISION MANAGEMENT METHODOLOGY

Fair Isaac uses a seven-stage, twenty-five-step methodology we have developed based on years of experience working with our clients to implement decision management technology. No matter the scale or scope of the project, these steps are required. As shown in Figure A.1, the methodology is a continuous loop that starts with strategy and ends in an operational environment that is monitored and in turn informs further refinements to strategy.

Here is an overview of the seven stages of the methodology:

Stage 1. Set Decision Strategy: Identify, assess, and link business objectives to decision improvements.

Stage 2. Identify Decision Yield: Determine critical decisions and potential decision yield.

Stage 3. Design Decision Architecture: Design the business architecture for your decision environment.

Stage 4. Build Data Environment: Develop and/or integrate the data environment required to inform decisions.

Stage 5. Build Mathematical Models: Develop and implement mathematical models to improve decisions.

Stage 6. Build Operational Environment: Develop, implement, and modify the operational environment to enable decision execution.

Stage 7. Continually Improve Decisions: Operate, monitor, and improve the decision environment.

Figure A.1 Decision Management Methodology

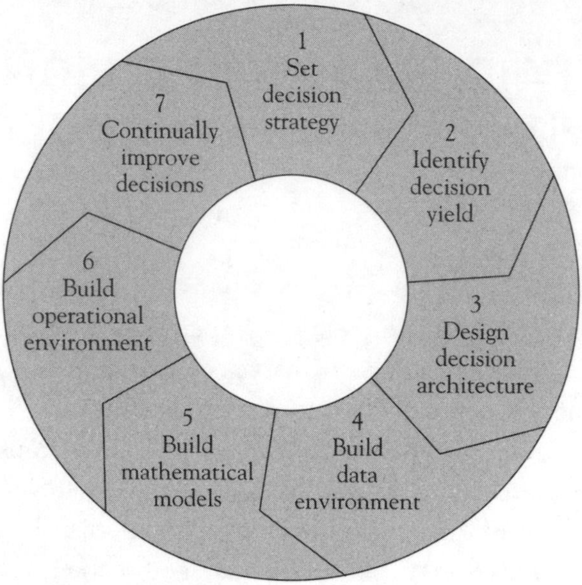

Source: Fair Isaac.

Details on each step of each stage follow; at the end of this appendix is a list of all the steps, for easy reference.

Stage 1: Set Decision Strategy: Identify, Assess, and Link Business Objectives to Decision Improvements

This stage consists of three steps that establish the strategic context and identify business opportunities in automating, improving, or connecting decisions.

Key Questions

- What are the possibilities?
- What are the important opportunities in alignment with company strategy or problems to be solved?
- What are the most important decisions related to these opportunities?
- How should opportunities be pursued based on priorities?

The purpose of this stage is for you to identify specific opportunities to pursue from a vast pool of ideas that your company can address through a strategic initiative and in terms of your specific decision-making environment. You should document and describe each opportunity in terms of its scope (for example, whether it is specific to a functional area or enterprise-wide). Next, you need to prioritize these opportunities and select which ones you will focus on. Then you need to develop a high-level plan for moving forward. This stage requires a high degree of management engagement (a highly regarded executive sponsor is paramount), strong project management leadership (a project manager and project analyst), and team collaboration.

Step 1. Identify and Prioritize Opportunities

In Step 1, you should conduct interviews and hold brainstorming meetings, making sure that someone synthesizes the information you collect during these interviews and meetings. Be sure to involve all relevant areas of the organization to be explored for potential opportunities. For any front-end planning project to be successful, you must ensure a high degree of candor in your interviews and brainstorming meetings. Teams must be willing to share openly about strengths and weaknesses and to identify strategies or capabilities that need to be developed or refined.

In all likelihood, certain ideas precipitated the project; these can provide a great starting point for further idea generation. Ideally you can then conduct a very broad level of brainstorming and discussions, where the project team gathers ideas (a.k.a. opportunities, pain points, problem areas, and the like) from an array of constituents. The project manager should identify the participants and establish the scope of this effort.

The areas you decide to explore should either pertain to customer strategy issues or relate to your overall customer-focused decision-making environment. The information gathering process can take many forms, including one-on-one interviews with key personnel and group brainstorming sessions. Although it is best to let interviewees and participants share openly, it may at times be necessary to subtly guide interviews and conversations. During the idea generation sessions, it is important to gather as much specificity as possible. For example, if someone says "It takes us a long time to respond to a customer prospect with a specific offer," be sure to understand the entire context for the comment. For example, ask follow-up questions such as these:

- Exactly how long does it take?
- For which product or product line is this an issue?
- Is this true irrespective of channel?

Next, you should review and discuss the interview write-ups and meeting minutes. Identify the key ideas, and translate them into a list of opportunity areas. Then compare your opportunity areas against each other, and combine them (if necessary) to eliminate redundancy. It is important at this point to circle back with key personnel and have them review the list of opportunities to ensure that it accurately represents their ideas. This is a critical step, in order to gain buy-in to the ongoing pursuit of these opportunities.

When it is time to select opportunities, sometimes the executive sponsor has the mandate to independently establish priorities. At other times a more democratic process may play out, with key stakeholders polled to rank-order the opportunities.

Step 2. Assess the Scope of the Opportunity

Your company may be facing certain hot issues that simply must be addressed. You may find too that other areas may surface that were previously not considered but represent high potential benefit. Finally, during this step, you should identify and select the most important and high-potential opportunities for further investigation.

Next, explore each opportunity area from Step 1 in detail. It is important to ensure a complete understanding of each opportunity and to follow up with personnel. Again, your scope should cover the reach *across* your organization (that is, either a specific functional area or enterprise-wide) as well as the reach *outside* the organization (for example, consider whether the opportunity involves partners or other third-party players).

This further breakdown will enable the project team to identify synergies and areas of overlap across the opportunity areas. Where the synergy is sufficient, you may be able to combine opportunities and expand them accordingly. This represents another area in which significant involvement is necessary— both to ensure that your assumptions going into the analysis are correct *and* to ensure that your company agrees that any combinations make sense. At this point, you must further analyze and assess each opportunity to establish what the team believes are the important or potential benefits. For example:

- This opportunity will lead to significantly improved turnaround time in making a specific offer to a prospect.

- Our ability to better segment our customer base will allow us to follow up on our mandate to become more customer-focused.
- Analytic improvements in this area can reduce the number of approvals requiring manual review by more than half.

These statements include a clear identification and description of the opportunity, an assessment of its root causes and effects, and the outcome expected if the opportunity area is pursued.

Finally, from the set of well-articulated opportunities, you must select the most compelling ideas. The prioritization done in Step 1, combined with the further analysis and synthesis from this step, will simplify this process. The sponsor again plays a key role, as he or she must have the wisdom to determine which opportunities will be most readily embraced by your organization and must inspire buy-in among key client stakeholders.

Step 3. Create a High-Level Plan to Address Opportunities and Scope

During Step 3, you need to compile all the elements of this first stage and translate them into a plan. You should define the work effort necessary to pursue the selected opportunities, and you need to recruit key stakeholders for the impacted areas to ensure their ongoing support and involvement.

This is a challenging step, because the opportunities usually represent change to the current way of doing things. Therefore, commitment from key leaders in the areas affected by the change is critical. It is important to ensure that these leaders assign quality resources from their respective areas to the project. The sponsor is an invaluable judge in this regard.

Next, the involved parties should collaborate to develop timelines. Your plan must accommodate the fact that ongoing business will be conducted in the midst of this new initiative. The planning effort must account for certain blackout dates when personnel in certain areas will be unavailable to the project due to other business demands. In other words, the total work effort in terms of person days must be spread across a timeline that recognizes the demands of each affected area.

You also need to divide each opportunity area into its component parts and describe each area in terms of the gap between the current state and the desired future state. Whether your focus is on a strategy or a specific decision-making process, this analysis must consider the necessary changes from a business process perspective, a technology perspective, and an organizational perspective. In addition, you must describe your strategic initiatives in reference to current statements of strategic intent and priorities, and you need to identify steps to ensure that you consider new strategic initiatives in that context.

Next, you need to obtain the buy-in and ongoing commitment of key stakeholders from the affected areas. Ideally, affected parties will already be familiar with the initiative through their involvement in interviewing and brainstorming meetings during Step 1. They must contribute to the planning effort by identifying resources they can commit to the project. You must ensure that a qualified leader for each affected area is chosen and that all such leaders get involved immediately so they own their aspect of the work plan and to make sure it well represents their area.

This involvement is important in terms of both the plan content and the plan timeline. It is important from a content perspective because only individuals from an affected area can know their specific environment, including their workload, their idiosyncrasies, and any exceptions to processes, policies, or decisions.

After you have developed the initial plan, recruited qualified members from each affected client area, and given those members the opportunity to modify the plan from their perspective, you should compile a final consolidated plan and submit it to the project sponsor for approval. You are then ready to move on to Stage 2.

Stage 2: Identify Decision Yield: Determine Critical Decisions and Potential Decision Yield

This stage consists of four steps to translate opportunity areas into a value proposition for the ongoing initiative.

Key Questions

- What are the important decision points?
- Who is making them?
- How are they made?
- What is our current decision performance?
- Can we improve decision making in this area?
  - Financial
  - Functional
  - Technical
- What improvements are possible?

Step 4. Create Decision Inventory and Business Process Flow
The purpose of this step is to document and gain insight into the way your organization currently functions, relative to the opportunity areas you're exploring. A starting point could be existing business-process design documentation, such as what may exist from a past process reengineering, CRM, or ERP project.

It may be harder for you to find previous inventories of decisions. However, business process flows often depict decisions as a branching point on the flow diagram, so any such documentation can again be a good starting point for you when you're creating an inventory of decisions.

In addition to reviewing preexisting documentation, you should also review the actual business procedures your company is following. This might include direct observation of the specific business environment you're analyzing (for example, you might visit a call center), but you *must* ensure that you directly involve key client representatives from each business area that you're exploring. When you provide them with a structured way to describe and document their business environment in terms of process flows, organizational roles, and decisions, that will lead to the most accurate and up-to-date answer.

4.1: Document High-Level Business Process Flows for Each Opportunity

Make sure this documentation is done at a high level, and use these documents to ensure that you have a complete understanding of the scope of the opportunity from a business process perspective.

4.2: Decompose the Opportunity Area into an Inventory of Decisions

Although most organizations understand and appreciate the importance of decisions, few organizations have described their operations in terms of decisions made. Therefore, in Step 4.2 you should carefully review the business process documentation from Step 4.1 to identify and create a comprehensive list of decisions made for each opportunity area you are investigating.

4.3: Document Organizational Roles and Decision Control

Finally, you need to identify all the individuals involved in each business process and decision, in terms of their role and decision-making authority—that is, you should clarify information such as:

- Who owns each process and decision
- Who has the authority to establish or change decision-making parameters
- Who executes the decision

The result is a consolidated picture of your current business environment. This deliverable depicts what the business environment looks like for each opportunity area, from a high-level business process and decision inventory perspective, and who the key players are, including a definition of roles, responsibilities, and decision-making authority.

Step 5. Identify and Design Pilot Models to Address the Objectives

In Stage 1 you may have identified a new or unusual application of analytics to a particular business problem, and before the project team can commit to delivering this analytic component, it may be necessary for you to confirm its viability by developing a pilot model. You should leave the level of modeling required for this assessment to the discretion of the analytic experts. Their assessment and final recommendation will determine whether a given analytic component can persist as part of the overall set of opportunities.

5.1: Identify Opportunities Requiring New or Unique Analytic Capabilities

Analytic experts should review all the opportunities identified for which analytic modeling is considered part of the solution. In unusual areas or in instances requiring more sophisticated techniques, the analysts may determine the need for further analysis, potentially including the creation of pilot models.

5.2: Design New Analytic Approaches for Select Opportunity Areas

For opportunity areas identified in Step 5.1 requiring additional analysis, you should explore and assess the analytic problem from each opportunity area. The analysts must assess their ability to create or improve analytics for each area in a cost-effective manner. It is important for the analyst team to distinguish between what is possible and what is viable. This step will confirm the viability of using analytic modeling to achieve the desired outcome. This includes ensuring that the modeling effort involved is both cost-effective and able to be integrated into an operational environment. For those areas determined to be viable for analytic modeling, you can use the pilot modeling to help quantify the potential benefit—most often expressed in terms of increased predictive precision or an improved decision strategy.

5.3: Make Final Recommendations

In Step 5.3, the analysts and the project management team must determine the best approach to take. The potential improvement must be great enough to justify any added investment and to offset any uncertainty in the proposed technique. This is the step in which final recommendations are made; you should quantify the potential improvements you're seeking and establish them as definite goals. You need to define the effort required to achieve your desired outcome, and you should especially highlight any unusual work effort and additional costs that may be introduced by the modeling techniques under consideration. In addition, you should identify any specialized tools or resources required as part of the new decision environment and carry these forward to subsequent steps in completing the business case.

Step 6. Capture Your Baseline Decision Yield

During Step 6, you need to assess each opportunity area from four perspectives: in terms of your business processes, your organization, technical aspects, and, of course, financials. You also need to consider, for each area, the decision yield factors of cost, speed, precision, consistency, and agility. Chapter Four covered these in detail; here's a quick refresher:

- *Precision* measures the accuracy of decision and process execution.
- *Consistency* measures the level of integration and coordination of decision and process execution across the organization.

- *Agility* measures the ability to readily respond to changing strategies and business conditions from a systems infrastructure and organizational perspective.
- *Cost* measures the effectiveness and efficiency of your decision-making or business process environment.
- *Speed* measures how quickly you can execute decisions or processes.

This baseline diagnostic establishes a quantitative assessment of current performance on each of these factors, combined with an assessment of the business impact of each factor in each opportunity area.

6.1: Analyze Current Business and Decision-Making Environment in Terms of Decision Yield

This substep involves completing a qualitative assessment for each opportunity area from a decision yield perspective. Here are some questions you should consider:

Precision

- How well do we know our customers?
- Is our strategic segmentation approach integrated into our operating environment?
- Is our customer segmentation granular enough to enable segment- or customer-specific treatment?
- Are we using analytic capabilities to enhance effectiveness? Are we making decisions using judgmental best practices, standardized rules, predictive models, or real-time optimization?

Consistency

- Who is making which decisions and who executes which functions? (Based on what criteria and authority? How consistently does this play out across channels, product lines, geographies, and so on?)

- How coordinated are our marketing activities across different product lines?
- Are our customers or prospects receiving conflicting messages from our organization?

Agility

- What is the impact of introducing new strategies into our operating environment? How much retraining is required? What modifications are required in our underlying systems infrastructure?
- Is our organization adept at assimilating change?
- What is the quality of our organizational communication vehicles?

Cost

- Are we making decisions through manual intervention or human review, or through scalable, automated rule systems?
- What is our sense of cost versus quality for this area, and what is the optimal balance?

Speed

- Are our customers being lost because of inefficiencies and slow turnaround times in our organization?
- How much time do we need to return a decision (say, on a request for service) to a customer or prospect?
- What is the potential gain of an incremental increase in system processing time for a decision?

Note: You may already have answered some of these questions in previous steps; the intent here is to ensure that you thoroughly assess each opportunity area in reference to each decision yield component.

6.2: Measure and Quantify Current Performance Using Decision Yield Diagnostic

This substep involves quantifying current performance for each opportunity area from a decision yield perspective. Some of these metrics are inherently numeric; the others can be quantified or graded on a 1 to 10 scale.

Precision

The level of precision is measured by:

- The accuracy with which business processes are carried out
- The accuracy of predictions
- The accuracy of decision logic (such as divergence from expected treatment)
- The level of granularity in business processes expressed and understood throughout the organization
- The level of granularity in customer or market segmentation
- The accuracy in projecting financial outcomes of decisions: profit, customer lifetime value, revenue, losses, and so on

Consistency

You can measure the degree of consistency by assessing

- The consistency of how you treat your customers across channels and across or within product lines, including
  - Your messages and offers
  - The decision criteria you use
  - Your customers' experience
  - The degree to which you use a full picture of the customer

- The consistency from a time-series perspective; that is, consistency of a given decision with those that preceded it
- The consistent understanding of each process across your organization—especially by your frontline workers who are called on to perform the tasks
- The systematic nature of your environment: for example, whether it is driven by rules in a software application or by individual discipline and training, or it is haphazard

Agility

You can measure the level of your company's agility by assessing

- How quickly your company can incorporate new information—such as regulatory constraints, changes in strategy, and changing business parameters—into your operating environment
- The number of resources required for your company to make a change to a business process or a decision strategy; for example, how well decision rights are understood and executed throughout your organization, and whether they are at the right level to reduce bureaucracy
- The time required for your company to make a change to a business process or a decision strategy—from design through implementation and training

Cost

You can measure the cost of decisions and business capabilities by assessing

- The activity-based costing of your processes and decisions
- The cost of information and data elements needed for your company to execute processes or decisions
- The cost of system resources

- The cost of labor—especially for manually intensive processes and decisions
- Any significant out-of-pocket costs, such as print and postage, third-party services
- Any lost opportunities

Speed

You can measure the speed of executing processes and decisions by assessing

- The elapsed time from step to step within a process flow
- The elapsed time between the request for a decision and fulfillment of that decision
- The elapsed time for batch or campaign runs

Step 7. Quantify Potential Improvements to Your Decision Yield

During Step 7, you need to identify specific areas for improvement and quantify them in terms of potential benefit to your organization. You should document the benefit as a value proposition that establishes the financial, functional, and technical goals for the initiative. You will also carry forward the specific areas for improvement—which you should state in terms of business requirements and corresponding goals—into the design phase (Stage 3), in which you will create a roadmap for making the specified improvements and envision your new business environment.

7.1: Identify Areas for Improvement

Use the decision yield diagnostic from Step 6 to generate the list of business requirements necessary to realize your desired improvements. You should state your requirements strictly in terms of *what* is needed—avoid describing *how* best to accomplish the requirement, as that will happen in the actual design steps.

Categorize your requirements in terms of five capabilities:

Analytics and Decision Logic

Here you should evaluate any form of mathematical, statistical, or rules-based capability to enable descriptive, predictive, or decision modeling analytics. For example, ask the following questions:

- How strong are the current analytic capabilities, and what new analytic capabilities are needed?
- What existing models are outdated and need updating or redevelopment?
- Are we periodically updating business logic based on market learning?
- What changes are required to improve the performance of our business logic?

Data Infrastructure

Here you should evaluate your internal and external data content requirements and your requirements for data access, timeliness, and accuracy. For example:

- What new information needs have we identified?
- Do we have the right information available at the point of need?
- What additional input data, internal or external, is required?

Strategic and Organizational Alignment

Here you should describe your need for alignment between your strategic priorities and your organizational execution. For example, ask the following questions:

- Is our operating environment aligned with our business strategy?

- Do we have the right skill sets and resources assigned to the most valuable priorities?
- What changes to organizational structure, roles, responsibilities, and requisite skill sets have we identified?
- What training and communication vehicles are required to ensure a successful and ongoing rollout of new initiatives and strategies?

Processes

Here you need to identify your new or modified business processes. Ask the following questions:

- What core business process changes or improvements have we identified?
- How will we manage these to ensure consistency, optimal performance, and agility?

Technology

Here you need to define areas in which you believe technology can enable improved performance—including modifications to your existing systems or descriptions of new tools and application areas. For example, ask what new or improved technical capabilities (tools, applications, and/or infrastructural components) are needed to achieve the benefit.

7.2: Quantify Potential Benefits

Assuming you've met the business requirements from Step 7.1—that is, you've quantified the potential benefits to your company against the baseline decision yield diagnostic you generated during Step 6—you need to consider what improvements you need to make in terms of each of the five decision yield components. You also need to establish your specific performance metrics and goals. These metrics and goals become the measuring stick against which you can gauge the ultimate success of the decision management project, which we'll cover in Step 22.

It is important for you to keep your improvements realistic—and to make a final assessment to ensure that the overall improvements are compelling enough to justify ongoing investment in this initiative. Therefore your executive sponsor should play a key role in making this determination and achieving buy-in from all your key stakeholders.

Stage 3: Design Decision Architecture: Design the Business Architecture for Your Decision Environment

The four steps in this stage create a blueprint for new capabilities that span technical, business process, and organizational elements of the decision environment.

Key Questions

- What are the best analytic methods to apply to our decision sets?
- Which specific decision areas (strategies, rules, processes) must we address?
- What capabilities do we need to create and modify?
- What organizational changes do we need to make in terms of roles, responsibilities, and structures?

During this stage you need to analyze your current environment from a business and a technical perspective. On the business side, this analysis should include a review of your current business guidelines, procedures, and processes. On the technical side, this analysis should include evaluation of your existing hardware, software, business applications, and databases.

Step 8. Determine the Best Analytic Approach

Although not every decision or project requires analytics, Fair Isaac has consistently found that analytics increases the decision yield in several dimensions, including these:

- *Precision*. Analytics enables much finer segmentation of individuals or transactions, often based on reliable forecasts of future outcomes that would be otherwise impossible.
- *Consistency*. Rigorous statistical analysis of data will always yield more consistent results than manual reviews.

- *Agility.* Analytics often provides a simple mechanism to rapidly change business strategy—for example, changing a score cutoff to include or exclude customers is a simple change with a quick and potentially significant effect.

- *Speed.* Analytics facilitates faster decisions by instantly sorting through masses of data to generate actionable insight and automate decisions by making this insight available as machine-readable metrics.

- *Cost.* Analytics can perform time-consuming analyses, meaning that staff are required to process only "gray area" or exception cases.

8.1: Assess Your Business Problem to Identify Analytic Opportunity

This step involves a fairly wide-open consideration of how you could use analytics to address your business problem. It is a good idea to consult with decision management experts to assess the opportunities.

Questions to ask in this step include the following:

- Are there data patterns that we could discover through analytics to increase the effectiveness of our decisions or the efficiency of our business processes?

- Could a forecast of future outcomes or customer behavior help us?

- Is manual review of data part of this decision or business process?

- Is the decision complex enough that modeling the results of these decisions could lead us to make better decisions?

8.2: Determine the Analytic Technology Approach

During any single project, several techniques can be used to analyze data, discover patterns and interactions, determine predictors, and develop a final model. The technology you choose will depend on several factors, including

- The business problem that you're concerned about (such as fraud, risk, marketing)
- The data you're analyzing
- The subject of analysis (such as individuals, transactions, or decisions themselves)

One, two, or all three of the basic analytic models may be appropriate for a given project:

- *Predictive model:* A type of model that rank-orders entities (typically customers or prospects) according to their likely future behavior. Examples include risk models, fraud models, and response models.
- *Descriptive model:* A type of model that classifies entities into similar profile groups. Unlike a predictive model, a descriptive model is not necessarily behavioral; it typically groups entities according to qualities or attributes. Its classification is also not hierarchical, unlike predictive or detection models, which rank-order entities.
- *Decision model:* A comprehensive model that determines the complex interaction between criteria used in a decision, the decision to be taken, reactions to that decision, and the objectives of a decision strategy. Decision models are used in optimization projects to help determine the ideal rules or strategy to maximize a given objective.

Step 9. Design Your Decision Environment

In this phase, you need to combine and synthesize the business requirements generated in your strategy and plan phase (that is, Stage 1) and then translate them into component designs—in terms of processes, rules, strategies, and applications.

Designing the decision environment requires an understanding of the existing business processes and how you can use analytic products and expertise to reengineer those processes to achieve your desired improvements. You should assemble or create process flow diagrams and text descriptions of your existing business processes and make sure you clearly identify problem areas or defects.

Working from these, the design team can then identify the enhancement requirements and produce an enhanced business process description that will indicate changes to the business processes themselves and how decision management components will be integrated to meet the requirements.

9.1: Describe Your Existing Business Processes, Including Known Problems and Defects

In this substep, you should create or refine detailed decision process flows, based on the results of the knowledge acquisition. Document your decision processes as diagrams and describe the workflow and application processing, showing the decision components involved and how they interact with human participants and other application components. By developing the existing process flows you will identify any breakdowns or defects and can then determine the requirements for enhancing the process and clarify how the enhancements will migrate to the new environment.

9.2: Describe the Enhanced Business Processes

Here you can derive your requirements for the enhancements to your business process from the problems and defects you've just identified, along with the business objectives and priorities you identified during Stage 2. You should then incorporate these requirements into an enhanced business process flow that shows how you will reengineer your existing processes to address those problems and deliver yield improvements.

Step 10. Design Your Decision Platform

Your decision platform design (that is, the technical infrastructure) must accommodate all of the following:

- The requirements for new components being added to the system (including application software and tools)
- Existing components that will remain or be reused
- Interfaces to data sources or other business systems
- Performance requirements for the new or enhanced system

Step 11. Define the Decision Management Roles, Responsibilities, and Decision Rights

A decision management solution typically involves roles and responsibilities that may be new to your organization, so you need to identify and define these. Define roles by using text descriptions, including the job title, a summary of the responsibilities, and the skills required. For example, these may include

- Analyst
- Data manager
- Model acceptance tester
- Rule architect
- Rule author

Other required roles may be familiar to your organization, but you may want to expand them, and they may require additional training; for example:

- Release manager for service updates
- QA tester for rules and strategy services
- Case analyst
- System administrator

For each defined role, you should specify which decision rights apply to decisions about creating or updating models, rules, and strategies.

Stage 4: Build Data Environment: Develop and/or Integrate the Data Environment Required to Inform Decisions

This stage consists of three steps to build out data sourcing, data flow, and data integration capabilities required to drive the decisions.

Key Questions

- What data do we have?
- What data do we need?
- How do we efficiently and effectively integrate the necessary data into our decision environment?

Complete, accurate data is essential to making precise, consistent decisions. The more complex a decision is—such as a mortgage lending decision, or a decision about whether a given transaction indicates fraudulent activity—the more important it is to have a rich, fresh stream of data available in real time.

Step 12. Design Data Flow: Sources and Sequences

The goal of this step is to understand the ideal data flow for your decision environment. You will then use this information to inform the data gap analysis in the next step and to guide collection and management of internal data as well as linkage to external data sources.

12.1: Identify the Data Required for Decisions Under Study

The following are considerations:

Source

Where is the data and who owns it? (This may also be relevant for internal data passed between departments.)

Cost

Does the cost of bringing this data into the client environment, or to a particular system for decision management, outweigh the marginal value provided by the data?

Availability or Attainability

- Can this data be accessed or acquired?
- Can it be made accessible to the right systems at the necessary times?

Timeliness or Freshness

How often is the data updated?

Coverage

- Will this data be available in every case and for every customer or transaction?
- If not, for what percentage of customers or transactions will it *not* be available?

Information Value

For modeling projects, does this data substantially add to the performance of the model?

Permission

Are there regulatory or legal restrictions on the use of this data, and does our company meet them?

Quality and Reliability

- Is this data accurate?
- What processes are in place to ensure that it is correct?
- What are the methods for identifying and correcting inaccurate data?

Of these measures, data quality—defined as any aspect of data that is associated with the usefulness of the data—may be the most difficult for you to determine. These quality aspects include typical traits that describe the data itself—such as cleanliness and predictive power—as well as elements that involve the delivery of the data.

When encountering a new external data source, the first step is to gather information on the data from the data vendor. You need to define and understand what data elements you're dealing with before you can use them for analytic purposes. Then you can receive a sample of the data, read it in, and verify it against the corresponding layout.

You can assess the quality of your data by examining the two main dimensions of data quality:

Fundamental Data Quality

This analysis involves investigating various descriptive qualities of the data, such as *completeness, cleanliness,* and *timeliness.* Here are a few guidelines:

- Evaluate the accuracy of your data by comparing it to similar data sets or certain benchmarks.

- Assess the match rates to see how well the data matches with other data sources.

- Examine coverage to ensure that the data is well representative of the pertinent population.

- Consider data storage, security, delivery, and cost, along with any legal limitations on the use of the data.

Predictive Data Quality

This analysis refers to determining how useful the data is for predicting a specific outcome. Here are a few guidelines:

- Assess the uniqueness of information in the data to determine how many distinct categories of information you can gain from the data.

- Investigate your ability to generate useful modeling characteristics from the data.
- Evaluate the information value for a case in which the data is used as a single source for predicting a certain outcome.
- Assess the marginal value for a case in which there are already existing data sources used for predicting a particular event.

12.2: Determine Requirements for Data Access

Data access involves both a systems aspect and a timeliness aspect:

- The *systems aspect* involves the format in which the data must be made available to the system or systems using it during a decision or process.
- The *timeliness aspect* involves determining when and how it must be accessed—for example, will you need to access the data (1) in real time while processing a decision or (2) in batch processing, wherein an entire set of records may be updated at once, outside of the processing of an individual decision?

12.3: Design Data Transactions, Stores, and Flows

This design should show how data will flow to and within your decision environment, including flows among your company's databases, external sources, the rules engine, and business systems such as campaign management, billing, transaction processing, or account booking systems. The data flow design should also consider data processing and conversions that must happen between systems and during transactions to ensure that the correct data is passed to the decision management application from other systems in the correct format, and vice versa.

Step 13. Assess and Address Gaps

Few companies have flawless systems for collecting, storing, accessing, and processing data. Therefore your project team should consider whether outsourced services would improve the quality, timeliness, and other data criteria. You should then define any gaps between the required data and the current available data, exploring issues like these:

- Are we using the best sources of external data?
- Are only partial customer records available for this decision?
- Are we appropriately collecting, logging, and storing data acquired through our transactions and interactions, both to guide later decisions we make and for reporting purposes?

Step 14. Map Connectivity to Third-Party Data Providers

Sometimes data is required from third-party providers, which requires further analysis of acquisition costs, contractual terms, and services level agreements. In this stage, the basic questions to be answered include the following:

- At what point in the process should we acquire and pay for the data?
- What should the contractual terms be to support long-term use?
- How do we integrate the necessary data into our decision environment, with sufficient service level agreements to meet our processing requirements?

Stage 5: Build Mathematical Models: Develop and Implement Mathematical Models to Improve Decisions

The three steps in this stage create specific analytic models for the decisions.

Key Questions

- How much can we improve our analytic performance?
- Which characteristics have the greatest impact on model outcomes?
- Is it operationally feasible?

Whatever the technology, methodology, and deliverables, the purpose of the models is to take in data and produce an actionable insight that you can use to improve decisions in your company. That insight may be any of the following:

- A better understanding of a customer's risk or potential
- A clear indication of fraud risk
- A better understanding about the relationship between entities such as your customers and your products
- A clear guide to how you can improve your business's rules and strategies to achieve better results

Step 15. Gather Data Required for Modeling

Data gathering is often the most time-consuming part of an analytic project. It is essential that your data be correct and complete and that you understand any known biases in the sample—and then correct or address those biases. Different models have different data requirements. For example, predictive modeling projects in retail banks need both *observation data* and *performance data* on the same group of accounts or transactions:

- The first set consists of data available at the time a decision is made; for example, application data collected when an applicant applied for a loan.
- The second set consists of data subsequently observed that indicates performance (for example, loan performance data from a year after the loan was booked). Many descriptive models do not forecast future outcomes, so performance data may not be necessary—for some of these models, you may need a more extensive set of external data.

For decision modeling projects, you will need a robust set of observation and performance data. This includes all the data available at the time of the decision being modeled, including the results of predictive and descriptive models. Your team will also require more data on the outcomes of decisions—including

- What decision was taken
- What the intermediate results were
- The final outcome (for example, profitability of an account)

Step 16. Build Your Models
The model development process is an interactive one in which your projects may involve multiple analytic technologies. Different steps are also required for different model types—for example, whether you use descriptive models, segmentation models, or decision models.

Step 17. Test Model Performance
In this step, your analytic team validates the model's performance to show that it is making consistent, correct, and precise predictions.

Stage 6: Build Operational Environment: Develop, Implement, and Modify the Operational Environment to Enable Decision Execution

This stage consists of three steps to create the software, organizational, and process capabilities required to integrate new decision making into operations. The software step integrates data, analytic models, and rules into a decision process that may be stand-alone or part of an enterprise software application. The organizational step focuses on overall structure as well as individual skill building. The process step adds to and/or modifies existing business processes in accordance with the overall design and objectives.

Key Questions

- What does it take to integrate decision rules, with consistency, into our business environment?
- Who owns the ongoing management and maintenance of our decision-making environment?
- Who has the authority to establish decision rules and parameters?
- Who needs to be trained in using these capabilities?

During this stage, you'll be creating and testing new software solutions (custom built based on software development tools or prebuilt yet configurable applications). You'll also design and implement organizational changes and begin training programs. Stage 6 ends when you've integrated your new capabilities into your company's business environment.

Step 18. Build Your Decision Management Application

In this step, you need to design and develop the required system components and then test them. The extent of this effort can vary greatly, depending on a number of factors, such as:

- The amount of custom development required
- Required modifications to your company's existing infrastructure
- The nature and complexity of your business's processes and rules

Step 19. Build Decision Rights: Organizational Structure, Skills, and Compensation

Implementing a decision management solution can often cause changes to your company's business processes and in turn necessitate changes to organizational roles and responsibilities. Therefore you should establish a change management leadership team, ideally with representatives from each functional area that will be affected by your solution.

As your company creates new capabilities, it is common to identify processes, structures, or policies that will soon become outdated and need to be redefined. You then will need to explore specific, detailed work tasks and define new ones. You must also make adjustments to your organizational structures and approval processes. Finally, you should assess your organizational policies, balance these against the goals and objectives of your decision management initiative, and modify them if necessary. All of these elements will introduce change into your organization, which will be more successful if you take into account these preparations:

- *Prepare your employees for change.* It is important to communicate with the employees who will be affected— and to do so early in the process. Even before specific answers are clear to you, you should make your employees aware of the initiative you are undertaking and let them know that change is coming. You should explain the rationale for the overall initiative to everyone to achieve buy-in and support.

- *Listen to the employees who will be impacted by the change.* Understanding employees' concerns presents two opportunities:
  - First, there may be legitimate issues that can be uncovered only by those most directly involved with the area under consideration.
  - Second, genuine two-way communication can often turn resistance into cooperation and cooperation into commitment to the new solution.
- *Identify new functional competencies.* You may need to define new functional competencies to support your new decision management solution. This is an important prerequisite to developing a training plan. In addition to training, you may also need to update your company's job descriptions and performance management systems to incorporate these new competencies.

Step 20. Roll Out Decision Processes and Rules

The culmination of the project occurs when you release the solution into the operating environment. You should migrate the tested and accepted technology components to your production environment, assign the people you've trained to fill their required roles, and activate your system monitors to ensure that the system performs properly and notifies the right people of any error conditions. A successful rollout is a crucial element in determining the satisfaction of the department or departments specifically involved in the project.

Stage 7: Continually Improve Decisions: Operate, Monitor, and Improve the Decision Environment

This stage consists of five steps to continually monitor the operational impacts of decisions, ensure that the decision yield benefits are achieved, and make any necessary adjustments to improve performance.

Key Questions

- Are we realizing the improvements we expected?
- Can we identify areas for additional improvement?
- Are there new decision areas we should address?
- Where and when do we invest to further improve our decision-making ability?

Decision management makes it possible for your company to improve your business's processes and results, but the benefits you realize will diminish over time unless you actively monitor and improve the decision-making environment. In many organizations, there's a tendency to "stick with what's working," which can result in a successful decision management environment that remains relatively static for too long. No matter how successful your initial implementation and how powerful your initial set of strategies, you should plan to continually update your strategies, models, and systems to gain maximum competitive advantage.

After all (as discussed in detail in Chapter Four), one of the central tenets of decision management is *adaptive control*: creating an environment in which to test, evaluate, and adopt new strategies in order to adapt to new market and operating conditions.

Step 21. Operate Your New Decision Environment

Once you've established your new decision environment, it will become part of your business's day-to-day operations. The processes required to operate it will vary depending on the nature of your specific environment, including the products and services you use and whether you've installed the decision environment internally or at an external service provider's site (for example, at a credit card processor).

Most decision environments have at their core an automated function for executing business rules or decision strategies. This requires business users to set up and modify business rules, which are automatically deployed after IT review. Some decisions will be only partially automated, and they will require business users to manage either a few exceptions (for example, decisions on individuals whose credit scores fall into a "gray area" right around a score cutoff) or a larger number of cases (when the decision environment is used to supply intelligence and guidance to business users who must take further action). A small percentage of decisions will be identified as requiring manual review; your system should be configured so it can route these decisions to staff (such as an insurance company's underwriting staff) before resuming the automated process.

Step 22. Confirm Realization of Your Decision Yield

This step is not meant to validate that the models or software are operating without error—you should already have confirmed that. Rather, in this step you should evaluate whether your company's use of the decision environment is producing the desired results you laid out during Stage 2, and whether the decision yield is the recommended metric.

It may take some months for you to determine the business impact. For example, there may be a learning curve in the use of the system, which means your desired reduction in required staff time will happen gradually. Similarly, you may have to measure customer performance over the course of months to determine whether decisions are having the desired effect.

Step 23. Identify and Implement Changes to Your Decision Environment

Although you can discuss and even begin to make additional changes before Step 22, in most cases you will need to see the benefits from the original or most recent project before you contemplate new projects. This step helps identify those new projects, using in-stream tests to determine if there are more creative ways to improve decisions by changing segments, decision strategies, analytic models, rules, or business processes. With the proper structure, those tests can be run in a production environment with limited impact on overall performance, while providing real performance data on the potential changes. If those potential changes look successful, they then can quickly be implemented more broadly.

Step 24: Feed New Knowledge Back into Your Decision Environment

As noted in Step 23, you can use your decision management environment to test new strategies and determine which are the most effective. This can lead to new understandings about the decision, which you can then implement by changing your business rules or decision strategies.

Better understanding of your internal business processes should lead to changes that will promote greater efficiency. This will include making sure that individual decision-making reflects, rather than refutes, the guidance provided by the decision management application.

This step often will involve designing and proposing a training curriculum for senior executives, business users, the analytic team, and IT staff.

Step 25: Identify New Decisions to Improve

During Stages 1 and 2, your project team may have identified other decisions that could benefit from decision management. These may have been identified when you evaluated your then-current (now previous) way of doing things and in the value proposition that was part of Stage 1. In addition, your project team may discover other decisions during the project itself. Here are some logical decision areas to investigate:

- Decisions in other areas affecting the customer relationship
- Decisions on other product lines
- Decisions in other departments
- Decisions in other geographical regions

During this step, you can use the same criteria that you used to evaluate opportunities in Stages 1 and 2 to prioritize new decision areas by the potential bottom-line impact of decision automation and analytics.

Summary of Fair Isaac's Decision Management Methodology

Stage 1: Set Strategy and Identify the Business Opportunity or Problem

Step 1. Identify and Prioritize Opportunities

Step 2. Assess the Scope of the Opportunity

Step 3. Create a High-Level Plan to Address Opportunities and Scope

Stage 2: Identify Critical Decisions and Potential Decision Yield

Step 4. Create Decision Inventory and Business Process Flow

Step 5. Identify and Design Pilot Models to Address the Objectives

Step 6. Capture Your Baseline Decision Yield

Step 7. Quantify Potential Improvements to Your Decision Yield

Stage 3: Design the Business Architecture for Your Decision Environment

Step 8. Determine the Best Analytic Approach

Step 9. Design Your Decision Environment

Step 10. Design Your Decision Platform

Step 11. Define the Decision Management Roles, Responsibilities, and Decision Rights

Stage 4. Build the Data Environment Required to Inform Decisions

Step 12. Design Data Flow: Sources and Sequences

Step 13. Assess and Address Gaps

Step 14. Map Connectivity to Third-Party Data Providers

Stage 5. Build Mathematical Models to Improve Decisions

Step 15. Gather Data Required for Modeling

Step 16. Build Your Models

Step 17. Test Model Performance

Stage 6: Build and Modify the Operational Environment to Enable Decision Execution

Step 18. Build Your Decision Management Application

Step 19. Build Decision Rights: Organizational Structure, Skills, and Compensation

Step 20. Roll Out Decision Processes and Rules

Stage 7: Continually Improve the Decision Environment

Step 21. Operate Your New Decision Environment

Step 22. Confirm Realization of Your Decision Yield

Step 23. Identify and Implement Changes to Your Decision Environment

Step 24: Feed New Knowledge Back into Your Decision Environment

Step 25: Identify New Decisions to Improve

Appendix B: Glossary

adaptive control system A software system that automates customer treatment decisions using champion/challenger testing to determine the better of two or more strategies. Adaptive control systems can be used for origination, account management, and collection functions, and they can make use of scoring models.

algorithm Mathematicians think of an algorithm as a series of mathematically derived instructions to accomplish a defined task. We further define an algorithm as a procedure for solving a problem mathematically in a finite number of steps that are often repeated. More simply, think of an algorithm as a recipe that if followed precisely yields the best result.

analytics Sophisticated mathematical and statistical processes, typically used to identify and summarize data patterns. We classify analytic techniques as *predictive modeling*, *descriptive modeling*, or *decision modeling*.

champion/challenger testing A process that applies an existing strategy (champion strategy) to the majority of a customer or prospect group, and another strategy (challenger strategy) to a segment of the group to identify the more successful strategy.

channels The distribution mechanism a company uses to interact with customers and prospects.

characteristic In a predictive model, this is a variable. It means specific information obtained from an application, credit bureau report, or internal billing file used to predict a future outcome; for example, "number of bankcard trade lines."

consumer behavior   The actual behavior of a consumer, such as inquiries, purchases, offers accepted, frequency of contact, and preferred channels.

consumer behavior database   A dynamic repository of true consumer behavior. It includes transaction rates, purchase "intents" (regardless of whether they are completed), survey information and preferences, and so on. This information is leveraged to create dynamic dialogues with a consumer that create value for that consumer and for the business.

data capture   A data processing term for the collection, formatting, and storage of data in computer memory according to predefined fields; for example, customer name, account number, and dollar amount of purchase.

decision agility   The ability to respond quickly to changes in customer preferences, competitive offerings, economic conditions, and regulatory oversight.

decision consistency   The ability to make coordinated, repeatable decisions across business functions, geography and time, and personnel and situations.

decision engine   The class of software that automates decisions by applying a business strategy or policy to a set of prospects, customers, or transactions.

decision environment   A company's systems, processes, resources, and personnel involved in making decisions.

decision management   The discipline of automating, improving, and connecting decisions throughout an organization, based on data, business policies, and desired outcomes. Decision management provides a new level of control over business decisions executed in application software and customer-facing operations.

decision model   A comprehensive model that determines the complex interactions among criteria used in a decision, the decision to be taken, reactions to that decision, and the objectives of a decision strategy. A decision model can be used to optimize customer treatment decisions.

decision precision The ability to select the optimal course of action in order to derive the maximum benefit from each specific customer, circumstance, or opportunity.

decision yield The sum benefit of improved and automated decision making resulting in increased revenue, reduced costs, and reduced risks as follows: making more profitable and targeted decisions (precision); in the same way across channels, business units, and geographies (consistency); while being able to adapt on the fly (agility); at reduced operating and development costs (cost); at real-time speeds that accelerate business processes (speed).

descriptive model A type of model that classifies entities using data, such as demographics, to cluster these entities into similar profile groups. It is typically used to segment customer populations. Unlike a predictive model, a descriptive model is not necessarily behavioral.

expert model A model developed based on analysts' or other experts' expertise and previous experience, as opposed to through empirical data analysis.

external data Third-party data purchased and gathered to make a more informed decision.

internal data Information generated by an organization's ongoing business operation.

predictive model A type of model that analyzes data to rank-order entities (typically, customers or prospects) according to their likely future behavior. Predictive models analyze past and present performance to predict how likely a customer is to exhibit a specific behavior in the future. For example, an attrition model measures the likelihood of a consumer to attrite or churn. This category also encompasses models that detect subtle data patterns to answer questions about customer behavior, such as fraud detection models.

rules management system Software used to manage, maintain, and change business rules that capture decision logic, company policy, or regulatory policy.

validation Any process that measures the validity of a statistical tool, such as a scoring model.

Acknowledgments

The decision to write a book begins with a vision. In our case, it was John's, because he took the lead to initiate this project, and he sketched the vision on one page. Larry provided an invaluable historical and forward-looking perspective. Two years later, with the assistance and support of many people, that single page has become *The Deciding Factor*.

We are especially indebted to our writing partner, Ann Graham, who traveled with us (figuratively and literally) to assist with the research and to tell the stories that bring the concept and the practice of decision management to life in this book. Joe LaLuzerne participated in many of our brainstorming sessions, and he provided invaluable research and interview support.

Many current and former Fair Isaac colleagues, from around the world, contributed generously of their time and ideas in interviews, chapter reviews, and ongoing support through e-mail exchanges, conversations, and introductions to sources. We are grateful to Mark Greene, Darcy Sullivan, Andy Jennings, Mike Campbell, Jeriad Zohgby, Eric Wells, Chisoo Lyons, Sally Taylor-Shoff, Scott Horwitz, Brad Jolson, Eric Educate, David Shellenberger, Ian Turvill, Jim Kalustian, Peter Bove, Barry Honeycombe, Craig Watts, Robert Duque-Ribeiro, Frans Labuschagne, Yen Chang, Jun Hua, Jane Johnson, Lynn Johnson, David Kropp, Gary Crays, Mark Eastwood, Alkis Vazacopoulos, Carlos Serrano-Morales, Shawna Morgan, Vance Gudmundsen, Bruce Harris, Bernhard Nann, Dan Sougstad, Jonathan Rotenberg, Mary Hopper, Joe Milana, Charles

Pangrazi, Marc Cohen, Raffi Kassarjian, Robert Hecht-Nielsen, Ray Boyle, Brian Kane, Craig Dillon, John Sandifer, and Damian Matich.

We also thank our clients who shared material about their companies for case studies: J. P. Martin (JPMorgan Chase Bank, N.A., Canada), Matt Smith (Best Buy), Mohan Jarayaman (ICICI), Brian Burdick (Dell Financial Services), and Elina-Sarno Politi (Bank Santander).

C. K. Prahalad, M. S. Krishnan, and Venkat Ramaswamy from the Ross School of Business at the University of Michigan; Chuck Lucier, senior partner emeritus from Booz Allen Hamilton, Inc.; Nigel Morris, cofounder of Capital One, Inc.; Gareth Herschel of Gartner, Inc.; Julia Johnson of IBM Global Business Services; and Bill Marquard of Marble Leadership Partners inspired our team to employ their ideas about strategy, competition, and information technology to enhance our discussion of decision management.

Art Kleiner, editor-in-chief of *strategy+business* magazine, and Bill Birchard, a writer and long-time collaborator with Ann, provided counsel and ideas, starting with the book proposal through the writing of the last pages of the manuscript. Our agents, Earl Cox and Lynette Khalifani of Earl Cox and Associates Worldwide, did a wonderful job helping us to write the book proposal. Kate Kane was an invaluable addition to the editing and writing team in the final days. Karen Murphy and Byron Schneider, our editors at Jossey-Bass, have been dedicated to making this book a success. Ann's father, Kurt Blumberg, provided knowledge of business before the digital age.

Last but not least, we thank our families and close friends, and particularly our spouses, Ann Nash, Diane Rosenberger, and Stephen Graham, for their patience, support, and encouragement.

John Nash and Larry Rosenberger

The Authors

Larry Rosenberger was named Fair Isaac's first research fellow in 2007, following more than thirty-three years of service to the company. In this capacity he continues to pursue research projects that advance Fair Isaac's analytic science. From 1999 to 2007 he led Fair Isaac's Analytic R&D Unit, focused on early stage innovation in exploratory, predictive, and decision analytics applied to helping Fair Isaac's clients in numerous industries. From 1991 to 1999 he served as president and CEO. During that time Fair Isaac experienced consecutive years of record growth, with annual revenues increasing from $31 million to over $276 million. Prior to that position he managed the Engineering, Research, and Development Division. In that capacity he was responsible for the technical development, production, and marketing of the company's most advanced products. Rosenberger holds a bachelor of science degree in physics from the Massachusetts Institute of Technology; in addition, he holds a master of science degree in physics as well as master of science and master of engineering degrees in operations research from the University of California, Berkeley. He is also chairman of the board of directors of the Buck Institute for Education and serves on a number of for-profit and other non-profit boards.

John Nash is Fair Isaac's vice-president of corporate strategy. He joined the firm in 2002 and has played a central role in the creation and growth of the company's vision for decision management. Prior to Fair Isaac, Nash was vice-president of product strategy for Seisint, Inc. (now a subsidiary of LexisNexis), an information products company specializing in risk management. In the 1990s, Nash was an associate partner at Accenture, where he founded the global Customer Insight practice, which focused on making fact-based customer decisions through improved data management, analytics, and business integration. Nash has worked with Fortune 500 companies in financial services, retail, consumer packaged goods, and high tech. Nash holds degrees in business from the University of Minnesota, with his MBA degree having a focus on information and decision sciences.

Ann Graham has spent her career as a journalist writing about management and strategy. She is a longtime contributor to and editor of *strategy+business* magazine, and she has been a writer and editor for *The Economist Group*, Gartner, Inc., Booz & Co., and *Knowledge@Wharton*.

Index

Coke's MyCoke Reward program, 60–62; creating value from customer data, vii; decision models for increasing, 140; evaluating customer's purchasing behavior, 45–46; humanizing customer segments, 46–49; Internet data and, 25; proprietary customer profiles for, 37; *See also* Reward programs

C

Canadian Tire, 87–88, 112
Capital One, 17–20, 22, 63–64, 85, 86, 101
Card Lab website, 64
Carte Blanche, 11–13
Cashless economy, 153–154
Cell-phone based consumer lending, 163–166
Cemex, 162
Center for Digital Democracy, 75
Center for Evidence-Based Medicine, 172
CepKredi, 164
Challenger strategy, 91–92, 93, 94
Champion strategy, 91–92, 94
Change: adopting customer-centric model, 44, 117–119; business strategy and, 145; identifying processes needed for, 204; implementing in decision environment, 223; making in operational decisions, 178–179; preparing employees for, 219–220; recruiting stakeholders for, 192–193; resistance to corporate, 113–115
Charge cards, 9, *See also* Credit cards
Chief decision officer, 111
Christensen, Clayton M., 23

Cinematch, 37, 41
Citibank, 13
CitiGroup, 165–166
Club of Rome, 4
Club Penguin, 160
Co-creation: customizing car loans, 66–67; defined, 63; developing products with, 63–64; opt-in/opt-out choices with, 70–71; privacy of data and, 65–66; social networking invitations and, 159–160
Coca-Cola, 59, 60–62, 75, 174
Cohen, Jack, 37
Commerce coalition, 154–155
Companies: aligning priorities, 203–204; automating decision vs. work flow in, 127–128; business titles in, 111–113; co-creating with customers, 63–67; competitive advantage for, 142–146, 161–168; conflicting objectives for, 93, 95–96; as constrained profit seekers, xvi–xvii, 88–89; creating feedback between data and actions, 123–124; decision management journey for, 80–82; decision-making styles, 124–125; defining and executing strategies within, 148; differentiating, 20–23, 143, 144, 149–150; disciplines for data use, 82–87; effect of digitization on, xi; execution gaps between data and action, 122–123; finding revenue base, 35, 51–53; handling data privacy, 71–72; how they think, 55–56; introducing predictive analytics to, 81; managing trade-offs, xvi–xvii, 178; organizational

INDEX 239

relevant loyalty programs for, 50; Tesco, 25–27, 34–35, 38–42

Customers: analytics for e-grocery, 39–41; balancing needs with profitability, 77; co-creating value with companies, 63–67; creating value from data about, vii; data privacy and, 57–58, 65–66, 71–74; data shared by companies, 154–157; expectations of, 27–28; exploring with descriptive analytics, 129–131; focusing on, 42–45; how they think, 55–56; humanizing segments of, 46–49; identifying high- and low-risk, 87–88, 89; predicting video selections, 26; purchasing behavior of, 45–46; questions focusing service on, 33–34; relevant loyalty programs for, 50; strengthening relations with, vii, xvii; support for classic department stores, 175–177; tracking behavior of, 153–154; unique shopping experiences for, 25–27; See also Customer segments; Personalizing customer experience; Reward programs

D

Daniel Yankelovich group, 58

Data: access to, 214; acquiring third-party, 215; addressing gaps in, 215; amassed by Cap One, 18–19; benefits of data mining, 121; building environment for, 187, 188, 211–215; captured with MyCoke Rewards, 61; co-creation and privacy of, 65–66; collected with Tesco Clubcard, 39–42; consumer responses to privacy of,

73–74; defined, ix; designing flow of, 211, 214; disciplining use of, 82–83; electronic medical records, 172–173; emergence of mass consumer, 13–20; execution gap between actions and, 122–123; exploring with descriptive analytics, 129–131; finding valuable information in, vii; gathering for mathematical models, 216–217; growth and costs of collecting, 23–25; handling sensitive, 71–72; Harrah's use of customer, 51–53; importance of using, x–xi; improving infrastructure for, 203; information architects' use of, 105; integrity when using, 75–76; measuring credit bureau, 17; obtaining from social networking sites, 158–161; organizational barriers to accessing, 115; security of, 57–58; sharing for common customers, 154–157; size of data sets, 22–23; from social networking sites, 158–161; strengthening customer relations with, vii, xvii; tapping into unstructured, 157–158; tracking consumer transactions, 153–154; using descriptive analytics with, 128–131; using Web browser, 25, 72; See also Analytics; Data environment; Privacy

Data environment: about, 187, 188; addressing data gaps, 215; considering data source and quality required, 211–214; designing data flow, 211, 214; key questions for, 211; requirements for data access, 214

Data General Nova, 15

We7, 63
Websites. *See* Internet
Webvan, 38, 40
Welch, Jack, 145
Wells Fargo Bank, 15
WestJet, 64

Work flow, 127–128

Z

Zealots, 73
Zopa, 171
Zuckerberg, Mark, 70